Fantastic Cats

Fantastic Cats

A FEAST OF FAMED AND FABLED FELINES

DESMOND MORRIS

First published in the United Kingdom in 2006 by Little Books Ltd,
48 Catherine Place, London SW1E 6HL

10 9 8 7 6 5 4 3 2 1

A CIP catalogue record for this book is available from the British Library.

ISBN 10: 1 904435 62 9   ISBN 13: 978 1 904435 62 4

Printed and bound in Great Britain by William Clowes Ltd, Beccles, Suffolk

CONTENTS

LIST OF COLOUR PLATES

Detail from *The Gods and Their Creators, 1878, by Edwin Long (1829-91)*. Sculptures and other artistic representations of the cat were widespread in ancient Egypt. *Courtesy of The Art Archive.*

A witch, like this one pouring a magic potion, was always accompanied by a black cat, thought to be a 'Familiar' in the service of the Devil. *The Love Potion, by Evelyn de Morgan (1850–1919. Courtesy of The De Morgan Centre, London.*

When the Earl of Southampton, was imprisoned in the Tower of London by Queen Elizabeth I, his devoted cat Trixie made its way across London and climbed down the chimney that led to his cell. Once there, it remained to keep him company until he was released, two years later. The Earl was so impressed with his cat's loyalty that he commissioned a portrait showing himself and his pet together in his cell. *Henry Wriothesley, third Earl of Southampton, and Trixie, in the Tower of London, c.1601–1603, by John Critz the Elder (1552–1642). Courtesy of The Bridgeman Art Library.*

Cardinal Richelieu owned fourteen cats. His pets were housed in a special room of their own. On his deathbed he left them a bequest in his will so that they would be cared for, but as soon as he was dead the animals were all slaughtered by the Swiss Guard. *Cardinal Richelieu and his collection of cats, from Les Animaux Historiques, based on the Letters of C G Leroy, by Ortaire Fournier, Paris, 1861. Courtesy of The British Library.*

Dick Whittington's famous cat is conscripted to work on *The Unicorn*, a ship plagued with rats and mice. *Dick Whittington handing over his cat to the captain, taken from Whittington and his Cat, Grant & Griffith, London, 1845. Courtesy of the British Library.*

Study of a tabby cat's head by the famous feline artist Louis Wain. *Study of a Tabby Cat, by Louis Wain (1860–1939). Courtesy of Celia Haddon and Bonham's London.*

The French novelist Colette (1873–1954) had a lifelong passion for cats, and wrote a number of books about her pets. *Sidonie Gabrielle Colette (1873–1954), with one of her beloved cats. Courtesy of Bettman/Corbis.*

Socks, the 'First Cat', belonging to Bill and Hilary Clinton. Their daughter Chelsea, 14, was reputed to have written a 'rap' song which included the words: 'Socks sucks, I hate that cat. Socks sucks, worse than GATT.' It later emerged that this was the work of anarchic leftist journalist, Tom Gargola. *Socks, the first cat of the Clinton family, 1994. Copyright Larry Downing, courtesy of Corbis.Sygma.*

In the 1961 New York romantic comedy *Breakfast at Tiffanys* starring Audrey Hepburn as Holly Golightly, her cat was called simply 'Cat'. The feline role was played by a ginger tom named 'Orangey'. *Holly Golightly played by Audrey Hepburn and 'Cat', from Breakfast at Tiffany's, 1961. Courtesy of The Kobal Collection.*

Cats have figured prominently in advertising campaigns for over a century, a high point being reached in the brilliant posters of Toulouse-Lautrec and Théophile Steinlen in Paris in the late nineteenth century. *Chat Noir, a poster advertising a cabaret, one of many by artist Theophile Steinlen (1859–1923). Courtesy of Dover Publications.*

In Lewis Carroll's Alice in Wonderland (1865) a large cat is encountered, lying on a hearth and grinning from ear to ear. Alice asks 'Please would you tell me why your cat grins like that?' The only answer she gets is: 'It's a Cheshire cat and that's why.' *Alice speaks to the Cheshire cat, by Lewis Carroll, taken from Alice's Adventures in Wonderland, Macmillan & Co, London 1890. Courtesy of The British Library.*

In *The Godfather* the tabby cat that Don Corleone was holding was a stray found by Marlon Brando. It was so grateful for all the attention it was getting, that it purred so loudly that it drowned out the lines from the other characters and they had to re-record their voices. *Marlon Brando in The Godfather (1972). Courtesy of Corbis.*

Felix the Cat, seen here sitting on a piece of cheese, was the first of the famous animated cartoon cats. He appeared as early as 1919 in *Feline Follies* for Paramount. *Felix the cat sitting on a piece of cheese, by Pat Sullivan. Courtesy of Blue Lantern Studios/Corbis.*

Donald Pleasance as the arch-villain Blofeld in the James Bond thriller *You Only Live Twice* (1967). The cat's name was Solomon. *Donald Pleasance and companion, taken from ou Only Live Twice, 1967. Courtesy of The Kobal Collection.*

The tough, outdoor, huntsman image created by American author Ernest Hemingway is strangely at odds with his private love of cats. The Hemingway house was overrun with no fewer than thirty pet cats. *The author Ernest Hemingway with Boise. Courtesy of The Ernest Hemingway Foundation.*

Arthur was hired by Spillers, the British petfood company in the 1960s because he could scoop his food out of a tin with his paw. Between 1966 and 1975 he appeared in 309 TV commercials. *Courtesy of Wood Green Animal Shelters and Dalgety Spillers Foods Limited.*

INTRODUCTION

CATS HAVE BEEN celebrated for thousands of years, as symbols, as literary characters, as much-loved pets, as show champions, as cartoon images, as television performers, as advertisement logos, and even, occasionally, as film stars.

It has to be admitted that, where movies are concerned, they have fared less well than dogs, because, of course, they are too independently minded to be pushed around by demanding film directors. An obedient dog will wag its tail happily and perform 'take five' of a difficult shot, but even a well-trained cat will start to wag its tail with an entirely different message at this point and will soon take the first opportunity to vacate the set. Film director Michael Winner once said he would never start on a new film that included a feline role unless he had seven identical-looking cats available to him right from day one.

Some cats become famous because of the work they do, but others have fame thrust upon them simply because their owners are famous. A cat living in the White House, or at No. 10 Downing Street, may in itself be a modest moggie with no particularly outstanding qualities, but because of its location, its doings often rate a mention in the newspapers or on television.

Fictitious cats have become famous over the centuries, from Dick Whittington's Cat

1

to Lewis Carroll's grinning Cheshire Cat to Hollywood's Felix and Tom and Jerry. Others have gained fame as the subjects of renowned artists, from to Klee and Picasso to Andy Warhol.

In this little book I have tried to bring together all the different categories of celebrated cats, to create a sort of 'feline hall of fame' where every cat that has ever become well-known rates at least a brief mention, from the very sad ones, like Thomas Hardy's faithful friend who ended up in a biscuit tin, to the wonderfully comic ones, like James Thurber's cat William, who thought that, when a ship was sinking, the cry that went up was 'William and Children First!'

1

FELINE TERMS

AILUROPHILIA

A TECHNICAL TERM meaning the love of cats. For further information on famous ailurophiles, see Chapter 5, Famous Cat Owners.

AILUROPHOBIA

The technical term for the fear of cats. Some ailurophobes cannot bear to be in the same room as a cat. Others can tolerate their presence, but cannot bear to be touched by them. Still others have a specific fear of a cat jumping up on them unexpectedly. Apart from these intense phobic responses, there survives in some regions a more general fear of felines because of their supposed mystical powers and their close relationship with witchcraft and the devil.

Intense ailurophobia is rare, but when it does occur it can cause untold misery for the sufferer. It may start through a childhood trauma – perhaps a sudden unpleasant shock involving a cat or a kitten. For the very small child, a kitten looks like a fluffy toy and there is a temptation for the infant to squeeze the little animal too tightly. When this happens a startling discovery is made: the fluffy toy has needle-sharp claws, pain-inflicting daggers that it had previously kept hidden. For the toddler this is so unexpected that, in a few cases, the experience can leave a mental scar. This traumatic memory can then develop into a full-blown phobia in adult life.

A second way in which cat phobia can arise stems from an irrational fear on the part of parents that the family cat may try to smother the newly arrived baby, by sitting on top of its face when the child lies sleeping in its cot. This old wives' tale is amazingly persistent, despite the fact that no cat could possibly relax and sleep, on top of a squirming, suffocating baby. As a result, many an infant may experience a shrieking mother rushing into the nursery and yelling at the cat to leave the room. These early associations between cats and panic may leave their mark and resurface later in the life of the child.

Strangely, studies of phobic reactions have revealed that women are far more likely to suffer from this affliction than men. This requires some additional explanation and it has been suggested by psychoanalysts that there may also be a sexual element involved. The cat has often been seen as a symbol of sexuality and it is possible that, in some instances, an intense fear of cats may reflect a suppressed sexuality on the part of the woman concerned.

The cure for cat phobia is straightforward enough, but distressing for the patient. It requires a series of step-by-step familiarization lessons, in which, at first, things only remotely feline are presented to the victim. These may be simply photographs of cats or kittens, or toy animals. After a while, a kitten is placed in a small, secure cage and left on the far side of a room, while the phobic person is gently reassured that it cannot get near. Gradually the animal is moved closer and day by day the phobia can be reduced in intensity until eventually the victim can actually hold a kitten. After this, the longer the sufferer spends in the company of cats the better, but always with the careful avoidance of any sudden unanticipated move. After a few months of therapy, it is usual for even the most intense forms of cat phobia to disappear.

Many sufferers wrongly believe that there is no cure and can never be one. For them there is a needless, lifelong fear of encountering a strange cat, a fear that sometimes ends with them refusing to venture out of doors at all. Their condition is beyond reason, but it is certainly not, as they believe, beyond cure.

For further information on famous ailurophobes, see Chapter 2, Feline History.

AILURUS

This is the ancient Greek name for the domestic cat. It is also spelled *ailouros*. It is said to have been coined by Herodotus, the Greek historian, when he first encountered cats during a visit to Egypt in the fifth century BC. He referred to them then as *ailuroi*, meaning 'tail-wavers'.

CAT

The English name for a member of the feline family. The name is similar in other languages:

Anglo-Saxon	cat/catt
Armenian	gatz/gadoo
Arabic	quttah/kittah/kitte/qitt/qutt
Basque	catua/catus
Bohemian	kot/kocour (m)/kote/kotka (f)
Breton	kaz
Bulgarian	kotka/kotki
Catalan	gat/cat (m)/cata (f)
Celtic	cat
Cornish	cath/kath/katt
Czechoslovakian	kocka
Danish	kat
Dutch	kat
Egyptian	kut
Finnish	katti
French	chat (m)/chatte (f)
Gaelic	cat
German	katze/katti/ket
Greek	gata/catta/kata
Hebrew (Sephardic)	chatool (m)/chatoola (f)

Hebrew (Ashkenazi)	chasul
Hindustani	katas
Hungarian	kaczer
Icelandic	köttr/kottur (m)/ketta (f)
Irish	cat/cait
Italian	gatto (m)/gatta (f)
Latin	catus/cattus ★
Lithuanian	kate
Maltese	qattus
Manx	cayt
Middle English	cat/catt/kat/katt
Middle German	kattaro
Modern Egyptian	kut (m)/kutta (f) ★
Norwegian	katt (m)/katta (f)
Nubian	kadis
Old English	gattus
Old French	chater
Old High German	chazza/chataro/cazza/caza
Old Norse	kött-r
Old Slavonic	kot'ka
Polish	kot/koczor (m)
Portuguese	gato (m)/gata (f)
Provençal	cat (m)/cate (f)
Prussian	catto
Russian	kot (m)/kotchka/koshka (f)
Scottish	catti
Slovenish	kot
Sorabian	kotka
Spanish	gato (m)/gata (f)
Swedish	katt (m)/katta (f)
Swiss	chaz
Turkish	keti/kedi/qadi
Ukrainian	kotuk
Welsh	cath/kath/cetti
Yiddish	kats/gattus/chatul

★ *see also next page: some languages have more than one word for cat*

6

Clearly, this is an ancient word that has spread across the world from a single source. The source appears to be Arabic, because the oldest use of it is found in North Africa. This fits with the idea that all domestic cats are descended from the North African Wild Cat, *Felis sylvestris lybica*, via domestication by the early Egyptians.

Languages that use a completely different word for cat include:

Arabic	biss (m)/bissie (f)
Chinese	miu/mio/mao
Dutch	poes
Filipino	pusa
Finnish	kissa
Hawaiian	owan/popoki
Hindi	billy
Hungarian	macska
Indian	billy
Indochinese	puss
Indonesian	kutjing
Japanese	neko
Latin	felis
Malay	kuching
Modern Egyptian	mau / mait
Mohawk	tako's
Rumanian	pisica
Sanskrit	mârgâras
Swahili	paka
Thai	meo
Vietnamese	meo
Yugoslavian	macka

In ancient Egypt the cat was known as *Mau-Maï, Maau, Maon,* or *Mau.*

CATERWAUL

Since Chaucer's day, the noise made by courting cats has been referred to as 'caterwrawling' or 'caterwauling'. It means, literally, 'cat-wailing'. The *Oxford English Dictionary* defines this word as 'The cry of the cat at rutting time.' Another dictionary calls it the cry of 'cats under the influence of the sexual instinct'.

Although it is true that the sound is most likely to be heard when cats are gathered for mating, it is misleading to assume that, because of this, its primary function is sexual. It is essentially an aggressive, threatening sound made by sexual or territorial rivals. Indeed, it may be heard at any time when two or more cats are fighting and may, on occasion, have nothing to do with sexual encounters. Even two spayed females disputing a territorial boundary can caterwaul as dramatically as any 'rutting toms'.

To human ears this is a disturbing sound and has been described as 'a discordant, hideous noise'. It consists of a series of rising and falling cries that vary from deep growls and gurgles to high-pitched wails and howls, as the intensities of the hostile interactions fluctuate from moment to moment.

CAT-FLAP

Cats hate doors. When a cat is indoors it always wants to be outdoors, and when it is outdoors it always wants to be in. To feel at ease, it needs to be able to patrol its entire domain at frequent intervals. Human doors are a hideous invention that robs it of this natural, territorial freedom.

It required a genius to solve this problem and fortunately one was at hand. No less a person than Sir Isaac Newton, the greatest natural philosopher of all time, considered the dilemma that faced his pet cats and, mindful of their comfort, promptly came up with the answer – a small cat-door set within the larger, human one. It is somehow apt that the great man whose laws of motion and gravity made him world famous should also have invented the cat-flap.

Newton has, however, been ridiculed for also inventing the kitten-flap. When his cat had kittens, he had a smaller hole made for them. Critics, who have pointed out that the great man was being silly, since the kittens could easily have passed through the main cat-door, are overlooking the fact that the tiny creatures may not have been strong enough to push up the larger flap.

Today, he would have been impressed to see the latest, high-tech cat-flaps that are available. These include electronically operated cat-doors which allow only the cat of the house to enter and exit. A small, battery-operated 'key' is attached to the cat's collar. As it approaches the cat-door, the flap automatically opens. After the cat has passed through, the flap closes and the door automatically locks itself shut. There are four settings: in only, out only, in and out, and fully locked. This system gives the owner complete control of feline movements and eliminates the shock of discovering a kitchenful of strays.

The cat-door appears to have been independently invented in Spain. It is reported that, in old Spanish houses there was a small hole, or *gatera*, to provide free passage for the domestic cats. These holes became well known as aids to human courtship. If the señorita's balcony was too high off the ground, the young lovers, when their parents refused to let them be together, would lie down on the ground, one on the inside and one on the outside of the *gatera*, to whisper their secret words of love.

CATGUT

Despite its name, catgut is not part of the guts of a cat. It comes instead from the entrails of sheep. Their intestines are prepared in a special way to make them into strong, flexible cords that have been used for centuries in making strings for musical instruments and for bowstrings.

There are three alternative explanations as to how sheepgut came to be known as catgut:

1   In Japan there is a traditional, three-stringed musical instrument called the *samisen*, which is shaped rather like a banjo. It is played by geishas to accompany songs. Unlike all other musical instruments, its strings are actually made from the intestines of cats. On one occasion the geisha girls, presumably saddened by the slaughter of cats for this purpose, held a ceremonial service for the souls of the felines that had met their end in the service of Japanese music.

There was also a bronze statue dedicated to these cats. It was erected in front of the great Buddhist temple to Nichiren in the Yamanashi Prefecture on the orders of the *samisen* manufacturers. One of the figures on the statue was designed to show a human form with a cat's head. Prayers were said there to appease the wrath of the departed felines and to ensure that they did not return to haunt those who killed them.

It is possible that knowledge of this unusual musical instrument filtered through to the West to give rise to the name 'catgut', but historically this seems unlikely.

2   In the seventeenth century, Italian violin-makers were using sheepgut to make their strings, but wished to keep their manufacturing techniques to themselves. To ensure that the source of their wonderful violin strings remained a trade secret, they gave out the false information that they were made, not of sheepgut, but of catgut.

3   The most popular explanation is that the sheepgut became known as catgut because of the noises made when it is plucked or scraped. At the beginning of the seventeenth century, one author wrote of fiddlers 'tickling the dried gutts of a mewing cat'. Later we read of a man upset 'at every twang of the cat-gut, as if he heard at the moment the wailings of the helpless animal that had been sacrificed to harmony'. These references come from a period when domestic cats were all too often the victims of persecution or torture, and the sound of squealing cats was not unfamiliar to human ears. These, and the typical caterwauling of mating cats, provided the obvious basis for a comparison with the din created by inexpert musicians scraping on their stringed instruments. In the imaginations of the tormented listeners, the inappropriate sheepgut became transformed into the appropriate catgut - a vivid fiction to replace a dull fact.

CATHOUSE

The slang term 'cathouse' has been used to describe a brothel for several centuries. Prostitutes have been called cats since the fifteenth century, for the simple reason that the urban female cat attracts many toms when she is on heat and mates with them one after the other. As early as 1401, men were warned of the risks of chasing the *cattis tailis*, or cat's tail. This also explains why the word 'tail' is sometimes used today as slang for female genitals. A similar use for the word 'pussy' dates from the seventeenth century.

CATNIP

Catnip, or Catmint, is the popular name given to a plant (*Nepeta cataria*) of Asiatic origin that has a powerful attraction for cats. Its appeal lies in a chemical called nepetalactone which is present in its stems and leaves.

When a cat finds this plant in a garden it may indulge in what has been described as a ten-minute drug 'trip'. It rubs and rolls on it, chews it, but does not attempt to swallow it. So intense is the response that the animal appears to be in a state of ecstasy.

Wild members of the cat family, including even the lion, react in the same way, but not every individual cat does so. There are some non-reactors and the difference is known to be genetic. A cat is either born a catnip junkie, or it is not. Conditioning and experience have nothing to do with it.

Young kittens do not show the response. For the first two months of life all kittens avoid catnip, and the positive response does not appear until they are three months old. Then they split into two groups: those that no longer actively avoid catnip, but simply ignore it and treat it like any other plant in the garden, and those that go wild as soon as they contact it. The split is roughly 50:50, with slightly more in the positive group.

The positive reaction takes the following form: the cat approaches the catnip plant and sniffs it; then, with growing frenzy, it starts to lick it, bite it, chew it, rub against it repeatedly with its cheek and its chin, head-shake, rub it with its body, purr loudly, growl, miaow, roll over and even leap in the air. Washing and clawing are sometimes observed. Even the most reserved of cats seems to be totally disinhibited by the catnip chemical.

Because the rolling behaviour seen during the trancelike state is similar to the body actions of female cats in oestrus, it has been suggested that catnip is a kind of feline aphrodisiac. This is not particularly convincing, because the 50 per cent of cats that show the full reaction include both male and females, and both entire animals and those that have been castrated or spayed. So it does not seem to be a 'sex trip', but rather a drug trip which produces similar states of ecstasy to those experienced during the peak of sexual activity.

Feline catnip addicts are lucky. Unlike so many human drugs, catnip does no lasting damage, and after the ten-minute experience is over the cat is back to normal with no ill-effects.

Catnip is not the only plant to produce these strange reactions. Valerian (*Valeriana officinalis*) is another one, and there are several more that have strong cat-appeal. The substance actinidine in the plant *Actinidia polygama* acts in the same way. The strangest discovery, which seems to make no sense at all, is that if catnip or valerian are administered to cats internally they act as tranquillizers. How they can be 'uppers' externally and 'downers' internally remains a mystery.

CAT-O'-NINE-TAILS

This was an implement of torture whose design was influenced by the idea that a cat has nine lives. It was a whip with nine cords, each cord having nine knots tied in it. As a result, every stroke inflicted a large number of small marks giving the overall impression of a body that has been clawed and scratched repeatedly by a savage cat. This type of whip was used as an authorized instrument of punishment in the British Navy and Army from the seventeenth century until it was finally outlawed in 1881. Its use was particularly brutal in the eighteenth century, when victims were given as many as 300 lashes, virtually flaying them alive.

The 'cat', as this whip was known in the navy, has given us the popular expression 'no room to swing a cat', meaning 'cramped quarters'. Some people imagine that this saying alludes to swinging a live cat around by its tail, but this is not so. It refers to the fact that the cat-o'-nine-tails was too long to swing below decks. As a result, sailors condemned to be punished with a whipping had to be taken up above, where there was room to swing a cat.

CAT'S CRADLE

Cat's Cradle is a game played by children in which a loop of string is wound back and forth over the fingers of both hands to create a pattern. Once the first child has created a pattern, the loop is transferred to the hands of a second child, creating a new pattern in the process. The loop is then handed back and forth repeatedly, making a different pattern each time. There are three rival explanations for the name 'Cat's Cradle' being given to this game:

1 The cradle formed by the string is the right size for a cat.

2 In Eastern Europe an old folk custom involved a live cat (as a symbol of fecundity) being secured in a cradle one month before a wedding took place. This cradle was then ceremonially carried to the newlyweds' house, where it was rocked back and forth in their presence. This, it was claimed, would ensure an early pregnancy for the young bride. A child's game could easily have developed from this ceremony, with its origins eventually forgotten.

3 Similar string games are played by peoples as far apart as Congo tribesmen and the Inuit, and these games have a magical significance. The string patterns are formed, altered and re-formed in the belief that these actions will influence the path of the sun. In the Congo this is done to persuade the sun to rest; in the frozen north it is just the opposite – the Inuit try to trap the sun in their strings to shorten its winter absence. The sun in these cases is envisaged as a 'solar cat', to be symbolically ensnared in the twisting string patterns. This 'solar cat' is reminiscent of the ancient Egyptian legend of the sun god Ra who, in his battle with the power of darkness, took the form of a cat. This equation between the cat and the sun is thought by some to have spread across the globe from culture to culture and to provide the true origin of the magical game of Cat's Cradle.

CATWALK

A catwalk is defined as a narrow footway or platform. It was originally used to describe a narrow footway along a bridge. Later it became a common term for a high walkway above a theatre stage, inside an aeroplane, or in various military contexts. Today it has become more associated with the narrow display area on which fashion models parade up and down. The question arises: why catwalk rather than a dogwalk, or some other name? The answer, according to Jean Conger in *The Velvet Paw*, is that: 'this name began at the bridge, and with the idea that puss would be very careful to make any bit of dry land hold his footsteps, because of his dislike of the water.'

GIB

This is an early name for a male cat. According to Charles Ross (1868) the name 'gib cat' or 'gibbe cat' preceded 'tomcat', especially in northern England. It was pronounced with a hard 'g'. It fell into disuse when 'tomcat' became popular, but was still employed in north-east England as late as the 1860s. The phrase 'gibbe our cat' is used by Chaucer in *Romance of the Rose*. Gibbe is also found in Shakespeare, where it refers to an old, worn-out animal.

Gib was a contraction of the name Gilbert that was also used for a male cat in earlier times. The Old French equivalent for Gilbert was Tibert or Thibert. Apart from 'gib cat', abbreviations sometimes employed for Gilbert and Tibert were 'gil cat' and 'tib cat'.

Another early name for a male cat was 'ram cat'. An alternative title was 'boar-cat', but both were replaced by 'tomcat' in the eighteenth century.

The French name for a tomcat is *matou*.

GRIMALKIN

This is a seventeenth-century word meaning 'a cat', especially an old female cat. It also came to stand for 'a jealous or imperious old woman'. Its oldest known usage is in the opening scene from Shakespeare's *Macbeth* (1605), where one of the three witches cries out 'I come, Graymalkin', implying that the cat was one of her familiars. This led to a definition of Grimalkin as 'a fiend supposed to resemble a grey cat'.

An early eighteenth-century definition describes the term as follows: 'Grimalkin to domestic vermin sworn an everlasting foe.'

The derivation of the word has been explained as follows: Grimalkin = Grey + Malkin. Malkin = Maud + kin. Maud = abbreviation of Matilda. Matilda = slang term for a slut. This makes the word Grimalkin = grey-slut-kin. Or, a grey being related to a slut. This may all be connected to the association of cats with witches, but there are few hard facts to go on.

Writing in 1969, Brian Vesey-Fitzgerald, who took special pleasure in debunking accepted wisdom, had no doubts on this matter, stating boldly: 'The true cat of witchcraft, the true familiar of the witch, was the grey cat, Grimalkin.' He rejects the widely held idea that, in the era of witch-burning, black cats were considered especially evil. He says: 'it is often stated that this was so and that many innocent old women were burnt or hanged at the height of the persecution because their cats were black. There is not a shred of evidence to support that allegation. It is true that many innocent old women were burnt or hanged, but this was not because their cats were black: it was simply because they had cats.' While it is true that all kinds of cats were persecuted during the witch-hunting years, the early illustrations of witches with their familiars nearly always do show a jet black cat, so it is hard to accept this view. However, it may well have been that grey-coloured cats, in addition to black cats, had a special role in the medieval annals of feline 'wickedness'.

KITTEN

In everyday speech the name 'kitten' simply refers to any young cat, but the technical definition varies from country to country. In Britain a domestic kitten is officially defined as a young cat up to the age of nine months.

In origin, it is thought that the term kitten derives from the general word for cat in the Turkish language, which is *keti* or *kedi*. Its earliest recorded use in the English language dates from 1377. The name Kindle is a special term for a litter of kittens.

The average number of kittens in a domestic litter is four. The record for the largest litter was nineteen, of which only fifteen survived. At birth, kittens measure about 13cm (5in) in length. They weigh about 115g (4oz). This will double in the first week. By the age of seven weeks they will weigh roughly 800g (28oz).

When they are born, the kittens are blind and deaf, but have a strong sense of smell. They are also sensitive to touch and soon start rooting for the mother's nipples. By day four, they have already started the paw-treading action which helps to stimulate the mother's milk flow. Their eyes do not begin to open until they are roughly a week old, and it will be another two weeks after that before they are fully open. By this stage they have started to crawl about and will soon be able to stand shakily on their small legs.

As they approach the end of their first month of life, they show the first signs of playing with one another. Whatever colour their eyes will be later in life, at this age all kittens are blue eyed and remain so until they are about three months old. Their teeth are beginning to break through at the age of one month. At roughly thirty-two days, they eat their first solid food, but they will not be weaned until they are two months old. (Wild cats take longer to

wean their kittens – about four months.) During their second month of life they become very lively and intensely playful with one another. Inside the house, pet kittens will use their mother's dirt tray by the time they are one and a half months old.

Play-fighting and play-hunting become dominant at the end of the second month.

In their third month of life they are in for a shock. The mother refuses to allow them access to her nipples. They must now make do entirely with solids and with liquids lapped from a dish. Before long their mother will be coming into oestrus again and concentrating on tomcats once more.

In their fifth month the young cats begin to scent-mark their home-range. They are shedding their milk teeth and exploring their exciting new world in a less playful manner. The chances are that their mother is already pregnant again by now, unless her human owners have kept her indoors against her will.

At six months, the young cats are fully independent, capable of hunting prey and fending for themselves.

MOGGIE

A non-pedigree dog is always referred to as a mongrel and, strictly speaking, this is the correct term for a non-pedigree cat, but few people use it in this way. They are much more likely to call their pet feline a 'moggie', sometimes spelt 'moggy'.

In origin, the term moggie began life as a local dialect variant of the name Maggie, meaning a dishevelled old woman. In some regions it was also the name given to a scarecrow and the essence of its meaning was that something was scruffy and untidy. By the start of the present century its use had spread to include cats. This seems to have begun in London where there were countless scruffy alley cats whose poor condition doubtless led to the comparison with 'dishevelled old women'.

By the inter-war period the word moggie had been abbreviated to 'mog' and in the 1920s and 1930s schoolboy slang referred to dogs and cats as 'tikes and mogs'. For some reason, this shortened form fell into disuse after World War II and the more affectionate 'moggie' returned as the popular term for the ordinary, common-or-garden cat.

PUSS

One of the colloquial names for a cat, thought to be derived from the Egyptian word *pasht*, but possibly taken from the Latin for a little boy, *pusus*, or a little girl, *pusa*. The Rumanian name for the cat – *pisica* – may have a similar origin.

The French equivalent of Puss/Pussy is *minet/minette*.

QUEEN

This is the term used for a female cat in the context of breeding. Breeders refer to their females as queens and their males as studs. In origin the word is said to be a debased form of the Saxon word, *wheen*, meaning the female sex. One of its earliest uses is in John Ray's writings in 1691, where the term wheen-cat is equated with queen cat.

The term has probably remained popular because it seems an appropriate title for a female who, when she is on heat, 'lords it over her males'. They must gather round her like a circle of courtiers, must approach her with great deference and are often punished by her in an autocratic manner.

STUD CAT

A stud cat is a male that is kept specifically for breeding purposes. The term is borrowed from the equine world where it originally meant a special place were horses 'stood' for mating. Over the centuries, 'stood' became 'stud'.

The term 'stud cat' was already in use by 1903, when Frances Simpson comments: 'STUD CAT. A male cat should not be allowed to mate under a year old, and if you wish to keep your stud in good condition do not allow more than two, or at most three, lady visitors a week.'

She goes on to say that: 'a really reliable stud cat is a very profitable possession… The usual fee for a visit to a stud cat is £1.1s' (approx $US2).

TABBY

The name is thought to be derived from *Atabi*, a type of silk manufactured in the Attabiah district of Baghdad where the manufacturers of silken fabrics were concentrated. The wavy markings of the watered silks resembled the hair pattern seen on the body of the striped tabby cat. It was exported to England in large quantities and on one occasion its striped patterns were compared with the markings on what was originally called the Striped Cat or 'Tiger' Cat. As a result, the breed soon became known as the 'Tabbi', which was later modified to Tabby.

2

FELINE HISTORY

ALLERGIES

THERE IS A LONG HISTORY of certain individuals suffering from severe allergic responses to cats. There are two schools of thought as to how this reaction originates. One sees it as a genetic weakness: a specific, inborn sensitivity to certain proteins which, when inhaled or ingested, even in minute quantities, create unpleasant physiological reactions. The other views it more as a psychological disturbance that begins in childhood and involves some kind of emotional trauma, unconsciously associated with a particular object. If that object happens to be a cat, then a serious allergic response may develop later in life.

Whichever of these explanations is the relevant one, the result can be all too real and extremely unpleasant, involving itchy eyes, runny nose, sore throat, headache, breathing difficulties and asthmatic attacks. Tests have shown that, in the case of a cat allergy, these symptoms are essentially a reaction to the animal's fur. To be more precise, it is a reaction to a mixture of shed hairs, cat's saliva and tiny particles of shed skin. This 'dander' or 'dandruff', when it floats in the air, is the almost invisible material that triggers the response in individuals who have this particular over-sensitivity.

Today there are two breeds which may avoid this problem, should an allergy-sufferer wish to become a cat-owner.

The first is the Cornish Rex Cat. The coat of this breed is short, sparse and curly and lacking in the usual long guard hairs. It is these guard hairs that appear to cause the allergic response in human sufferers, so when the Cornish Rex was first discovered it was hailed as the new answer to allergy problems. Several sufferers who tried keeping these cats reported delightedly that this was indeed the case, but it remains to be seen whether this works in every instance. Some allergy sufferers are much more sensitive than others.

For extreme cases there is always the Sphynx Cat from Canada. This is an almost naked cat and even the most sensitive allergy sufferers would be unable to generate much of a reaction to this remarkable animal. All it shows on its body surface is a short, soft down in place of the usual fur and, as the cat grows to adulthood, this down persists only on the animal's extremities. It is therefore covered with what looks like a suede or velvet coat and which, to the touch, feels like warm, soft moss. Providing the ultra-sensitive allergy sufferer or asthmatic would-be cat-owner owns a house with central heating, this bizarre new breed of cat is clearly the best answer at present.

Before long a new solution may be available. Research has been carried out by a on a cat-allergy vaccine called Catvax. Unlike other allergy vaccines in the past, Catvax promises to be permanently effective after only a few injections and to have no side effects. The original intention was to have it on the market by 1997, a putting an end to the frustrations faced by allergy-sensitive individuals who long to own a cat. Sadly, as often happens with new drugs under development, it ran into difficulties and the research is still continuing today. With any luck it will be commercially available in the near future.

BLACK CAT

In folklore, the all-black cat plays a special role. In earlier centuries, when cats were being severely persecuted by the Christian Church, it was always black cats that were singled out for the most savage treatment. All cats were considered to be wicked, but *they* were considered to be especially fiendish. This was because they were strongly associated with the Devil – the Prince of Darkness – who was believed to borrow the coat of a black cat when he wanted to torment his victims. So, when the Church organized annual burning-cats-alive ceremonies on the day of the Feast of St John, the most depraved of 'Satan's Felines' were strongly preferred and all-black cats were eagerly sought out for the flames.

Writing in 1727, Moncrif comments: 'It is true that the colour black does much harm to Cats among vulgar minds; it augments the fire of their eyes: this is enough for them to be thought sorcerers at the least.'

These victimized cats had to be totally black to be really evil in the minds of the pious worshippers. Any touch of white on their black coats might be taken as a sign that they were not, after all, cats consecrated to the Devil. As a result of this distinction, cats that were totally black became less and less common, while those that were black with a touch of white survived. Religion acted as a powerful selection pressure on feline colouration. This is the reason why today so many black moggies (as distinct from pedigree 'Black Shorthairs') have a small patch of white hairs somewhere on their body – often on the chest or around the whiskers. This patch, thought to be a sign of innocence, was given the name of 'Angel's mark' or 'God's finger'.

The fear of all-black cats as agents of the Devil also led to a common superstition that has survived to the present day. In Britain

it is said that if a black cat crosses your path this will bring you good luck. This is based upon the idea that evil has passed you by – it has come close but has not harmed you, hence you have enjoyed a moment of good luck. In North America a different superstition exists. There, a black cat signifies bad luck, on the principle that it is an evil spirit and therefore dangerous merely by its presence.

CAT HATERS

It is important to make a distinction between ailurophobes and cat haters. True ailurophobes, such as Napoleon, had a cat phobia: a deep-seated *fear* of cats. If this did lead them to become cat haters, the hatred was secondary. Their primary response was panic in the presence of a feline. But many other historical figures, who have lacked this terror, have nevertheless detested cats. Famous cat haters include the following:

Julius Caesar (100–44BC) The mighty Emperor is said to have held cats in horror.

Wu-Chao, Empress of China (624–705) The Empress hated cats and had them banished from her palace for a special reason. A lady-in-waiting she had condemned to death took her revenge, before she died, of issuing a threat that, in the afterlife, she would turn the Empress into a rat. Then she, the lady-in-waiting, transformed into a spectre cat, would hunt her down and torment her.

Pope Gregory IX (1147–1241) He initiated the feline holocaust in Europe that was to continue right through the Middle Ages and beyond. In a Papal Bull of 1233 he denounced the black cat as diabolical, thereby giving his official blessing to the widespread persecution of cats – already occurring locally in Europe – and set the course for five centuries of cat hatred, torture and burning.

Pope Innocent VII (1336–1415) In the early fifteenth century, this Pope added his voice to the persecution of cats, stepping up the onslaught, resulting in millions more feline deaths.

Pope Innocent VIII (1432–1492) Another pious Pope who failed to live up to his name. In his Bull of 1484 he condemned witchcraft and dispatched inquisitors to try witches and destroy them.

He made a particular point that the witches' cats were to be burned with them. He was persuaded to issue his Bull by two Dominican friars from Germany called Kraemer and Sprenger, names that should go down in history as the cat's worst enemies.

Henri III (1551–1589) The French King lost consciousness if he set eyes on a cat, and it is said that during his reign he executed 30,000 cats.

Elizabeth I (1533–1603) A feature of the Queen's coronation procession was a huge wicker Pope filled with live cats which was wheeled through the streets and then set on fire, so that they 'squalled in a most hideous fashion' as they burned to death. In origin this was, of course, symbolic cat hatred. It does not imply that the Queen personally hated the cats as animals. She was simply following the custom of the day of persecuting cats as agents of the Devil. But for the cats concerned, this was of little comfort.

William Shakespeare (1564–1616) Unhappily for those who respect both cats and Shakespeare, the majority of the bard's references to felines are vilifications. For example, in *All's Well that Ends Well*: 'I could endure anything but a cat, And now he's a cat to me… A pox upon him! For he is more and more a cat.'; in *Cymbeline*: 'Creatures vile as cats…'; in *The Merchant of Venice*: 'Some that are mad if they behold a cat.'; in *Much Ado about Nothing*: 'What though care killed a cat.'

King Louis XIV (1638–1715) In 1648, the French Monarch, crowned with a wreath of roses, ignited the fires and then danced around the pyres of cats being burned alive at the Midsummer Gala in the Place de Grève in Paris. He was a callous ten-year-old boy-king when this happened, and later reformed.

Buffon, George Louis Leclerc, Comte de (1707–1788) In his 1767 *Natural History* he described cats as follows: 'The cat is an unfaithful domestic, and kept only from the necessity we find of opposing him to other domestics still more incommodious, and which cannot be hunted; for we value not those people, who, being fond of all brutes, foolishly keep cats for their amusement...' He adds that cats 'possess... an innate malice and perverse disposition, which increase as they grow up, and which education teaches them to conceal but not to subdue. From determined robbers, the best education can only convert them into flattering thieves. ...they have only the appearance of attachment or friendship.'

Abdul Hamid (1725–1789) The Grand Sultan of Turkey who flourished at the end of the eighteenth century felt a real terror of cats.

Napoleon Bonaparte (1769–1821) One night after the Emperor had retired to his bedroom, he was heard screaming for help. When one of his aides rushed in, he found the great man in a state of panic, sweating profusely, and thrashing around wildly with his sword because a cat was hiding behind a tapestry.

Johannes Brahms (1833–1897) It has been claimed that the composer disliked cats so much that he used to shoot them with arrows. His assaults are supposed to have begun after the Czech composer Antonin Dvorák gave him a Bohemian Sparrow-slaying Bow. Brahms is reputed to have taken aim from his apartment window in Vienna and, if we are to believe an account by Wagner: 'After spearing the poor brutes, he reeled them into his room after the manner of a trout fisher. Then he eagerly listened to the expiring groans of his victims and carefully jotted down in his notebook their antemortem remarks.' According to Wagner, Brahms then worked these sounds into his chamber music. Some authorities believe this account of brutal cat-slaying to be true, but others insist that it was no more than a scurrilous slander on the part of Wagner, who is known to have disliked Brahms intensely.

Hilaire Belloc (1870–1953)   The Anglo-French author, writing about cats in 1908, said: 'I do not like Them… when one hears Them praised, it goads one to expressing one's hatred and fear of Them… so utterly lacking are They in simplicity and humility, and so abominably well filled with cunning by whatever demon first brought Their race into existence… All that They do is venomous, and all that They think is evil…'

Isadora Duncan (1878–1927)   At Neuilly in France, Isadora Duncan, the revolutionary American choreographer and dancer, lived next door to a countess who ran a cat sanctuary. The cats were constantly invading her garden and since, surprisingly, she detested felines, this drove her to extreme measures. The great dancer ordered her staff to hunt them down and drown them. At the height of this persecution the distraught countess found the corpse of one of her rescued strays hanging by a cord from the wall that divided the two properties.

Dwight Eisenhower (1890–1969)   During his occupancy of the White House, the American President banished all cats. He hated cats so much that he instructed his staff to shoot on sight any they spotted in the grounds.

Apart from these famous names, Ida Mellen, writing in 1946, reports that one of the world's greatest cat haters was a Chicago banker by the name of Rockwell Sayre. In the early 1920s, he started a campaign to rid the entire world of cats by the year 1925. Using the slogan 'A Catless World Quick' and distributing a verse that began: 'Who kills a cat gains a year, who kills a hundred never dies', he offered financial incentives to cat killers (ten cents each for the first hundred and $100 (£55) for the person who killed the last cat on Earth).

Cats, he said, are 'filthy and useless' and it was 'toadying to depravity to keep a cat around the house'. He claimed to have been inspiration for the killing of seven million cats during the first three months of his campaign, but was dismayed to discover that, when 1925 eventually arrived, there were still some left. He then decided to extend his purge for another ten years but, happily for the cat population, he himself was soon dead.

Note: In order to make cat haters seem as loathsome as possible, some authors have added the tyrants Hitler and Mussolini to the list, but there seems to be little evidence for this. Mussolini was in fact a cat lover who owned a splendid Persian Cat, and his daughter always took breakfast with her pet cat sitting on the table, even though it had long since died and been stuffed.

Bibliography

1940, Mellen, I. *The Science and Mystery of the Cat.* Scribner's, New York.

1963. Cole, W and Ungerer, T. *A Cat-Hater's Handbook.* W H Allen, London.

CAT ORGAN

In the days when cruelty to cats was an accepted form of public entertainment, there were several loathsome inventions to facilitate this callous pastime. One of these was the Cat Organ. This consisted of an instrument designed to make music from the terrified cries of a group of captive cats. One of these was paraded through the streets of Brussels in a procession that took place in the year 1549 in honour of Philip II. In involved a live bear, twenty cats and some monkeys:

'In the middle sat a great bear playing on a kind of organ, not composed of pipes, as usual, but of twenty cats, separately confined in narrow cases, in which they could not stir; their tails protruded from the top and were tied to cords attached to the keyboard of the organ; according as the bear pressed upon the keys, the cords were raised, and the tails of the cats were pulled to make them mew in bass or treble tones, as required by the nature of the airs. Live monkeys … danced to the music … Although Philip II was the most serious and the gravest of men, he could not refrain from laughter at the oddity of this spectacle.'

Sadly for animals concerned, the cat organ became a popular spectacle and improvements were made. The cords attached to their tails were replaced by 'spikes fixed at the ends of the keys, which prodded the poor animals, and made them mew piteously'. This form of feline torture remained in vogue for at least a hundred years, but

A cat organ, from an illustration of 1883

eventually disappeared and was replaced by strange feline musical performances. A poster from the late seventeenth century depicts a French cat-showman with his performing cats, some reading music, others playing musical instruments. It is not clear how he managed to make them sing or play, but it seems likely that he used some kind of pain to provoke the sounds. The difference now was that the pain was hidden rather than obvious, so that the onlookers could enjoy the strange 'concert' without being confronted by the conspicuously obvious animal torture of the infamous Cat Organ.

CAT RACING

Competitive cat racing seems highly improbable as a serious sport, but in the nineteenth century it did take place annually in Belgium. The manner in which it was organized does not reflect well on the Belgian attitude towards their feline friends at the time. In the first major cat book ever published (in 1889), Harrison Weir quotes a publication called *The Pictorial Times* of June 16th 1860: 'Cat racing is a sport which stands high in popular favour. In one of the suburbs of Liège it is an affair of annual observance during carnival time... The cats are tied up in sacks, and as soon as the clock strikes the solemn hour of midnight the sacks are unfastened, the cats let loose, and the race begins. The winner is the cat which first reaches home, and the prize awarded to its owner is sometimes a ham, sometimes a silver spoon. On the occasion of the last competition the prize was won by a blind cat.'

Cat racing resurfaced briefly in England in the 1930s. In a brave bid to imitate greyhound racing, a cat racetrack was opened in 1936 at Portisham in Dorset. The competing cats were set to chase an electric mouse, which they pursued down a 220-yard (202-metre) course. Another display of organized cat racing was apparently staged in Kent in 1949. Not surprisingly, both enterprises were dismal failures and serious cat racing has never been attempted again.

HOWEL THE GOOD

In the year 936, the then Prince of Wales, Hywel Dda, now generally known as Howel the Good, made himself famous in feline history by introducing special laws to protect domestic cats. This is a rare enough event at any time in human history, but in tenth-century Europe it was truly remarkable. Howel clearly felt, with good reason, that an animal of such value to agriculture, in its role as a pest controller, should be more highly respected. He therefore introduced a scale of prices for kittens and cats and fixed penalties for stealing or killing a cat. The prices varied according to the animal's age and killing skills: '1. The worth of a kitten from the night it is kittened until it has opened its eyes is a legal penny. 2. And from that time, until it shall kill mice, two legal pence. 3. And after it shall kill mice, four legal pence.'

The rules laid down by Howel the Good were so precise that, if a cat failed to kill mice, or if it was a female that failed to rear its kittens, the buyer could claim back one third of the price paid for it. And the penalties for killing or stealing a cat were, to say the least, imaginative: 'The worth of a cat that is killed or stolen; its head to be put downwards upon a clean even floor, with its tail lifted upwards, and thus suspended, whilst wheat is poured about it, until the tip of its tail be covered; and that is to be its worth; if the corn cannot be had, a milch sheep with her lamb and her wool, is its value; if it be a cat which guards the king's barn.'

The cat's value was also equated with that of other livestock: 'There are three animals whose… lives are of the same worth: a calf; a filly…; and a cat…' Sadly, this sensible respect for an important working animal was soon to be eclipsed by the savage superstitious persecutions of the Medieval Christian Church.

KATTESTOET

In the Belgian city of Ypres there is a curious Cat Festival on the second Sunday in May, called the *Kattestoet*. It is curious because it originated in an epoch when cats were suffering severe persecution and involved extreme cruelty to them, whereas today this same ceremony, with minor but significant modifications, is seen as a festival to celebrate the cat and is attended by thousands of cat lovers.

In its earliest form it consisted of a feast, the culmination of which was the throwing of live cats from the top of the tall tower in the city centre. The crowd cheered as the cats fell to their deaths because the unfortunate animals were seen as devilish creatures and the pious Christians who took part in these events felt that, by destroying the cats, they were defeating the Devil. Astonishingly some of the cats survived their great fall and managed to crawl away after they landed. This started a new superstition. If a cat survived, it must have been an innocent one and its charmed life meant that there would be a good harvest that year.

Amazingly, these cruelties persisted until the nineteenth century and were not stopped until the year 1817. In the 1930s, the good citizens of Ypres were missing their annual festival and it was decided to start it up again, but this time using only dummy cats. Abandoned during World War II, the Festival of Cats was not begun again until the 1950s and since then has grown and grown both in scale and popularity until today it is a major spectacle – a feline Mardi Gras. In fact, it has grown so big that it can no longer be held annually, but only at intervals of three years.

One of the modern festivals – the 37th in the modern phase – was held on Sunday, May 7th, 1994. The official festival programme for that day gives a flavour of the events:

11.00 hrs	Aperitif Concert
14.00 hrs	Introduction to the Parade
15.00 hrs	37th Cats' Parade begins
18.00 hrs	Cat Throwing (Belfort Tower)
20.30 hrs	Evening spectacular: 'Witches Brew', including Witch Burning in the Great Market
22.30 hrs	Grand Musical firework display

The parade is now so vast that it takes three hours to pass. It consists of enormous feline floats and cat effigies representing every phase of the cat's long history, starting with Cat Worship in Ancient Egypt and ending with a lively display by modern 'Cheercats' (young females with feline make-up, complete with cheerleaders' costumes and pom-poms). The giant floats are accompanied by thousands of adults and children, dressed as cats of one type or another, with marching bands and orchestras to serenade them. Although many of the towering cat figures are antique and impressively atmospheric, the combination of ancient cat persecution and modern cat celebration has about it a peculiar contradiction, as though Walt Disney had been asked to mount his version of the Spanish Inquisition.

The many floats included the following set-pieces: The Cat in Egypt, The Cat in Celtic Times, The Cat in Germanic Times, Cat Proverbs, Tybaert the Tomcat, Puss-in-Boots, Because of the Grease, A Bird for the Cat, They are Burying a Big Cat, Catty Kwabette and the Emperor Karel, The Siege of the Cat's Stronghold, The Condemnation of the Cat and the Witch.

The final burning of the witches may today be purely theatrical, but it is a sobering thought that it is re-enacted on the very spot in the city where, between 1561 and 1595, 300 witches were, in reality, brought to face the Inquisition and a hideous death in the flames.

MARRIAGE

It may be hard to believe, but there have been occasions when a formal marriage ceremony has been conducted for pairs of cats. In his *First Pet History of the World*, David Comfort reports that 'Dawn Rogers, a California Pet Pastor, ordained in the Universal Life

Church, performed seventeen marriage ceremonies for dogs, cats, horses, goldfish and frogs in 1986.'

One small advantage of being a cat owner, rather than a dog owner, was that the cost of a feline wedding was only $300 (£165), compared with $500 (£275) for canine nuptials.

MUMMIFIED CAT

Millions of domestic cats were mummified and buried in ancient Egypt. In the earliest times, this process was uncommon and special but in later periods it became routine and the cat mummies were 'mass-produced'.

The oldest known example of cat burials dates from the XIIth Dynasty (1991–1778BC). In a tomb at Abydos there were seventeen cat skeletons thoughtfully supplied with a row of milk dishes. Later, in the XVIIIth Dynasty (1567–1320BC) Prince Tuthmosis provided his beloved pet cat, Tamyt, with a magnificent limestone sarcophagus. The inscriptions refer to her as Osiris, the Lady Cat, indicating how highly she was valued by her owner. The writing on the lid informs us that she wishes to become an 'imperishable star' – in other words, that she hopes to ascend into the heavens. To help her along on her great journey, she is supplied with a roast duck on a table in front of her. Clearly this was a special cat of a special man and her treatment was exceptional. But it does show that, even at this very early date, pet cats were revered, if not actually deified.

About a thousand years later, the situation had changed radically. At this stage there were mass burials and literally millions of mummified cats were laid to rest, carefully wrapped in linen bindings and often wearing specially made feline masks. These have been found at many sites throughout Egypt and reflect a widespread practice of making votive offerings to the cat goddess, Bastet.

A drawing of a wall painting from the burial chamber of Tuthmosis III.

Once such a cat was buried, it became an intermediary between its owner and the gods, operating a ghost-cat information service to let the gods know about the prayers and needs of the earthbound human citizens.

Because these mummified cats were so helpful in solving personal problems by persuading the gods to listen to the needy, it followed that a much-loved family pet cat did not always die at the best moment. This little problem was neatly solved by the priesthood at the holy temples who, in effect, became feline factory farmers. They established 'dead cat supermarkets' near to the great shrines, where they kept vast numbers of sacred felines.
These they bred, housed, fed, reared to near adulthood and then systematically killed, embalmed, and encased in suitable wrappings for the pious pilgrims to purchase on their visits to the cult centres.

The scale of this operation must have been enormous, its organization and execution elaborate. At times, the demands of the believers were so great that, even with their careful planning, the priests could not keep up with the demand. Pondering this problem, it occurred to them that, since the faithful always bought carefully wrapped mummies of cats, they would never know precisely what was inside the wrappings. So they started to cut corners. X-ray examination of surviving cat mummies reveals that some of them were made up of cats' skulls with human bones, or cats' bones mixed up with those of jackals, birds or even reptiles. One 'cat' mummy was made entirely from frog bones.

Clearly, there was a commercialism bordering on the cynical in this priestly industry. What was worse, none of these cats had been allowed to enjoy a long life.

Examination of their teeth reveals that most of them were either between two and four months old or between nine and twelve months old. Only 4 per cent of them were over two years old when they 'passed away'. The way they passed was also rather suspicious. Many had had their necks broken; some had been strangled; and still others had been drowned.

Hundreds of thousands of cats died and were mummified in this way in a country where paradoxically the cat was sacred, revered and worshipped. We read of whole families going into deep mourning when the family cat died, of the imposition of the death penalty for 'murdering' a cat, and of a Roman soldier being stoned to death because he killed a cat. This may well reflect the attitude of the ordinary populace, but it certainly did not reflect the conduct of the crafty priesthood. Either the ordinary believers were ignorant of the priestly cat industry, or they knew about it but somehow managed to develop a mental double-standard, seeing the killing of temple cats as 'sacrifices' rather than murders.

Whatever the truth of these matters, one thing is certain; all along the Nile from Thebes to Bubastis, cat burials took place on a staggering scale. One cat cemetery alone was almost a kilometre long. In 1888, an Egyptian farmer, digging up a piece of land that had not been cultivated before, discovered 300,000 cat mummies. These were sold as fertilizer to British buyers. One consignment of nineteen tons, made up of the mummified bodies of about 80,000 cats, was shipped to Liverpool in England, where it was auctioned off at £4 ($7.20) a ton, to be spread on local fields, to encourage the crops to grow. It is said that, during the sale, the auctioneer used the body of one of the embalmed cats as his gavel.

This bizarre and undignified end to the story of the Sacred Cat of Ancient Egypt has a final, intriguing twist. On the farming land all around Liverpool, from time to time, Egyptian jewellery is brought to the surface by the ploughs of bewildered farmhands. Beads, scarabs and other small decorative artefacts that once adorned the mummified cats lie scattered there, awaiting the watchful eye, though few of the finders have the faintest idea how they came to rest on the cold alien soil of northern England.

POPES

The Vatican's attitude towards cats has varied from savage cat hating to gentle cat loving. Sadly, the overall balance has been against cats. Several Popes have issued instructions that led to the torture and slaughter of millions of innocent felines, whereas the few cat-loving Popes have only shown affection towards their own personal pets. Six Popes appear in the feline literature. They are:

Pope Gregory I (540–604). Reputed to be a cat lover, but the true ailurophile may have been a hermit who identified with the Pope.

Pope Gregory IX (1147–1241). Issued a Papal Bull in 1233 declaring black cats diabolical, initiating centuries of cat hatred.

Pope Innocent VII (1336–1415). Demanded an increase in the persecution of cats, leading to millions of feline deaths.

Pope Innocent VIII (1432–1492). Issued a Papal Bull in 1484 insisting that witches and their cats should both be burned to death, causing widespread suffering.

Pope Leo XII (1760–1829). His beloved cat Micetto was born in the Vatican. He was raised by the Pope and was often seen nestling in his robes.

Pope Pious IX (1792–1878). His pet cat waited patiently while his master dined, after which the Pope himself would serve a special meal to the animal, at the Papal table. Despite this, he refused permission for the opening of an animal protection office in Rome on the grounds that: 'men owed duties to his fellow men, but none to the lower animals.' His legacy, regarding animals, is summed up by the following passage from the Catholic Dictionary of 1897: 'They (animals) have no rights. The brutes are made for man, who has the same right over them which he has over plants and stones... it must also be lawful to put them to death, or to inflict pain upon them, for any good or reasonable end... or even for the purpose of recreation.'

RODENT SCARERS

In Europe as late as the eighteenth century, cats were regularly being placed inside the walls of new houses as a way of supposedly protecting the buildings against invasions by rats and mice. It is unlikely that these unfortunate cats were deliberately walled up alive in hollow cavities, to achieve this form of symbolic pest control. Recent studies suggest that this was not the case, and that they were dead before being immured in this way.

Several examples of these early rodent scarers, or 'vermin-scares', have come to light where it is clear that a cat was 'prepared' before being sealed up. The cats in question were carefully posed, often with a rat or a mouse placed in the mouth. Sometimes a bird was used in the role of prey. These manufactured cat-catching-rodent tableaux were probably sold to new house owners as magic cures for rodent infestation, and carefully placed in a wall cavity before the house was occupied. In some cases they were placed under floorboards or doorsteps.

Examples of these rodent scarers have been found in the London area, in both Bloomsbury and Southwark, and also in the Tower of London during renovations there in 1950 in an area untouched for 200 years. They have also been unearthed at a cottage in Essex, where a cat and her kittens were found plastered into a wall; in a medieval building at King's Lynn in Norfolk; in Cambridge, during building work on an old wall in 1811; in Dublin, where one was found hidden behind the organ in Christchurch Cathedral; in France, at an old charnel house in Rouen; and in Switzerland in the walls of a house at Rans, in the canton of Saint-Gall. In addition there is an example from Gibraltar, put in place by Spanish masons. And in Sweden one was found under an entrance in a house constructed as recently as 1920.

The strangest case concerns a 300-year-old mummified cat found hidden in an old house in Sudbury in Suffolk. When this building was being converted into a hotel in the early 1980s, the cat was removed, but there then followed a series of disasters including two fires and a structural collapse at the very spot where the cat had been walled up. In the face of this ill-fortune, ancient superstition once again reared its head and the owners had a special, glass-topped casket made for the cat and re-buried it near its original resting place. Sunk into the floor of the hotel lounge, visible to any visitor who wishes to inspect it, the cat once again protects its ancient site. At the re-opening of the establishment, now called the Mill Hotel, a priest was called in to perform a special blessing ceremony, and since then there has been no further mishap.

THERAPY

Studies of the effects that pet cats have on their owners have revealed that sharing a home with these animals is significantly therapeutic. In short, cat owning is good for your health. There are two reasons:

First, it is known that the friendly physical contact with cats actively reduces stress in their human companions. The relationship between human and cat is touching in both senses of the word. The cat rubs against its owner's body and the owner strokes and fondles the cat's fur. If such owners are wired up in the laboratory to test their physiological responses, it is found that their body systems become markedly calmer when they start stroking their cats. Their tension eases and their bodies relax. This form of feline therapy has been proved in practice in a number of acute cases where mental patients have improved amazingly after being allowed the company of pet cats.

Most cat owners feel somehow released by the simple, honest relationship with their cat. This is the second reason for the cat's beneficial impact on humans. It is not merely a matter of touch, important as that may be. It is also a matter of psychological relationship which lacks the complexities, betrayals and contradictions of human relationships. We are all hurt by certain human relationships from time to time, some of us acutely, others more trivially. Those with severe mental scars may find it hard to trust again. For them, a bond with a cat can provide rewards so great that it may even give them back their faith in human relations, destroy their cynicism and their suspicion and heal their hidden scars.

And a special study in the United States has recently revealed that, for those whose stress has led to heart trouble, the owning of a cat may literally make the difference between life and death, by somehow helping to reduce blood pressure and calming the overworked heart.

WARFARE

Surprisingly, there are reports that cats have been used in warfare on a number of occasions. The first dates back two and a half thousand years to the time when the Persians were at war with the Egyptians. Knowing that the Egyptians revered the cat and considered it to be sacred, the Persians developed the idea of a 'feline armour'. When their advance guard was making a hazardous push to secure a new stronghold, the Persian warriors went forward carrying live cats in their arms. (One authority suggests that the live cats were not carried, but attached to their shields.) Seeing this, the Egyptian soldiers were unable to attack them in case they accidentally killed one of these sacred animals. For them, such an act of violence against one of their animal deities was unthinkable. Indeed, if any one of them had killed a cat, even in these special circumstances, he would have risked being put to death. So in this way the Persians were able to advance with ease and the Egyptians were helpless to retaliate.

The second example appears much later, being illustrated in Christopher of Hapsburg's book in the year 1535. He was an artillery officer and in his report to the council of One and Twenty at Strasbourg he described the way in which 'poisoned vapours were shed abroad' by means of cats. The  unfortunate animals apparently had poison bottles strapped to their backs, with the openings pointing towards their tails. They were then sent off towards the enemy, running panic stricken, this way and that, and in the process spreading poisonous fumes. Christopher of Hapsburg was clearly a man of delicate sensibilities, for he added the comment: 'This process ought not to be directed against Christians.'

The third example dates from World War I, when the British government was fearful about the use of lethal gas by the Germans. They drafted 500 cats and sent them up to the front to be used in the trenches (in the same way that canaries had always been used down the mines) as chemical 'detectors'. Because the cats were much more sensitive to approaching gas than their human companions, they would act as an early warning system. If the cats suddenly collapsed and died, it acted as a signal that trouble was imminent for the troops. Whether any of these unfortunate cats ever saw England again is not on record.

The fourth example comes from World War II. During the terrible siege of Stalingrad in 1942, a cat called Mourka was used to carry messages about enemy gun emplacements. These dispatches had to be taken across a street that was alive with sniper fire. For a target as large as a human body, the short journey would have meant almost certain death. Mourka's tiny form stood a much better chance. And he had a good reason to make the trip: half-starved like everyone else in Stalingrad at the time, he knew that the company kitchens were situated inside the house to which the messages had to be taken. With this knowledge, he was never reluctant to make the perilous dash through the danger zone. Mourka rapidly became a hero, celebrated in the world's press. *The Times* of London paid him a special tribute in a leading article, ending with the words 'he has shown himself worthy of Stalingrad, and whether for cat or man there can be no higher praise.'

During the blitz on Britain, pet cats seemed to develop an uncanny awareness of impending attacks. One animal, nicknamed 'Bomber', could always tell the difference between the sound of RAF and German aircraft. When a Nazi bomber was approaching, the characteristic throbbing noise of its engines sent the cat scurrying for its personal shelter. Because of its sensitive hearing, it could be used as an early warning system for its human companions. This was not an isolated case, and there were several instances where the quick reactions of cats saved the lives of whole families. Seeing their cats dashing for cover, people would hurriedly follow suit, gaining the safety of shelters just before the bombs started falling.

Naval cats were also prominent in World War II. On board the beleaguered warships they doubled up as rodent destroyers and as lucky mascots. The most famous was a cat called Oscar who saw service with both the German and the British Navy. He started out as the much-loved mascot of the famous German battleship *Bismarck*. When this vessel was sunk in 1941, he managed to escape and was seen swimming among the wreckage by a British sailor who rescued him and took him on board the Royal Navy destroyer HMS *Cossack*. Five months later, the *Cossack* itself was sunk. Again Oscar survived and was transferred to the aircraft carrier *Ark Royal*. When *Ark Royal* was torpedoed by a U-boat, Oscar was rescued yet again. With three of his nine lives gone, it was decided to retire him to a sailors' home, where he quietly lived out his days in a less violent and much drier environment.

As sailor Charles Hodgson remarked, a ship's cat 'could create an oasis of peace and serenity, even amidst the noise and clamour of war'. Which makes one fear for the sanity of the inmates of the British Admiralty who, in 1975, dismayed sailors everywhere by banning all animals from HM ships.

Finally, in even more recent times, American military advisers suggested using the cat's excellent nocturnal vision to assist their troops as field guides during jungle night patrols in Vietnam. Training was begun and, in 1968, a platoon of military guide cats was shipped out to the Orient to play their part in the Vietnam War. The cats could hardly believe their luck. The night-time jungle was alive with exotic rodents and as soon as the cats were released they set off in hot pursuit. The American soldiers did their best to keep up with them as they scattered in all directions, racing through the undergrowth. Those cats that were kept closer to hand satisfied themselves by stalking and attacking the dangling pack straps of the soldiers immediately in front of them. The only consolation to be gained from this bizarre experiment was that, when the Viet Cong heard of this new American secret weapon, it is likely that several of them died laughing.

(Sadly, it has to be admitted that this last example of the use of cats in warfare was reported by a humorist called Brian

he delivered her to the captain; "for now," said Dick, "I shall be kept awake again all night by the rats and mice."

Those who were present, laughed at Dick's strange article for adventure: but Miss Alice, who felt pity for the poor boy, gave him some half-pence to buy another cat.

This and many other instances of kindness

McConnachie, who was writing for the satirical magazine, *National Lampoon*, a fact that was overlooked by several gullible authors in recent feline publications.)

Bibliography

1873. Duparcq, De La B. (Editor) *Les Chats de Guerre*. Paris. (Includes: *Chats de guerre antiques*; *Chats de guerre modernes*; *Chat de pontonniers*; *Chats maritimes*.)

WITCHCRAFT

Religious bigots have often employed the cunning device of converting other people's heroes into villains, to suit their own purposes. In this way, the ancient horned god that protected earlier cultures was transformed into the evil Devil of Christianity. And the revered sacred feline of ancient Egypt became the wicked, sorcerer's cat of medieval Europe.

In the same way, Freya, the Viking Goddess of Love, became a loathsome witch, and her faithful cats became the despised witch's familiars. Anything considered holy by a previous religious faith must automatically be damned by a new religion. In this way began the darkest chapter in the cat's long association with mankind. For centuries it was persecuted and the cruelties heaped upon it were given the full backing of the Church.

During this bleak phase of its history the cat became firmly linked in the popular mind with witchcraft and black magic. As late as 1658 Edward Topsel, in his serious work on natural history, followed detailed descriptions of the cat's anatomy and behaviour with the solemn comment that 'the familiars of Witches do most ordinary appear in the shape of Cats, which is an argument that this beast is dangerous to soul and body.' (The last

An illustration from Topsel's History of Four-footed Beasts and Serpents *(1658)*

execution of a cat for witchcraft in England was in the year 1712.)

The earliest record we have of this superstitious belief dates from the tenth century when, in the year 962 at the city of Metz (now in north-east France), the ceremony of 'Cat Wednesday' took place on the second Wednesday in Lent. This involved the burning alive of hundreds of local cats on the grounds that they were 'witches in disguise'. This was the start of a period of appalling feline persecution that was to last for eight centuries. There was, however, one period of respite following the Crusades. When the Crusaders returned to their European homelands they brought with them, in the holds of their ships, the dreaded Black Rat, and cats were suddenly in great demand to control this scourge. But the Christian persecutions were soon to resurface. In the thirteenth century, Papal might was brought to bear against supposed sorcery and unspeakable atrocities were inflicted on innocent humans and felines alike.

Worse was to come. The reign of terror for witches and their cats was further intensified in the fifteenth century and did not decline until as late as the eighteenth. Records show that in the sixteenth and seventeenth centuries, 100,000 witches were legally executed in Germany, 75,000 in France and 30,000 in Britain. Wherever possible cats were destroyed with them. The total slaughter of domestic cats must have run into the hundreds of thousands.

Because the cat was seen as evil, all kinds of frightening powers were attributed to it by the writers of the day. Its teeth were said to be venomous, its flesh poisonous, its hair lethal (causing suffocation if a few were accidentally swallowed), and its breath infectious, destroying human lungs and causing consumption. All this created something of a problem, since it was also recognized that cats were useful 'for the suppressing of small vermine'. Topsel's compromise was to suggest to his readers that 'with a wary and discreet eye we must avoid their harms, making more account of their use than of their persons'. In other words, exploit them, but do not get too close to them or show any affection.

This restrained attitude did, at least, enable farm cats and some town cats to live a tolerable life as unloved pest controllers, but for certain village cats life was far more unpleasant. If they happened to attach themselves to an old woman who lived by herself, they were risking a savage death as a witch's familiar. The sad irony of this unhappy state of affairs was that these animals played a comforting role in the lives of such old women. Any elderly crone, who happened to be ugly or misshapen enough to have repelled all potential husbands, and who was therefore forced to live a solitary life with no children of her own, often as an outcast on the edge of the village, would have been desperately in need of companionship. Maltreated cats, finding themselves in a similar plight, might have approached such women, who befriended them as substitutes for human companionship and love. Together, they would have brought one another many rewards and the kindness of these old women towards their cats was excessive. Anyone teasing or hurting their beloved felines might have been cursed and threatened. All that was required then was for one of these tormentors to fall ill or suffer a sudden accident and the old 'witch' was to blame. Because the cats wandered about, often at night, they were thought to be either the supernatural servants of the witches, or else the witches themselves, transformed into cat shape to aid their nocturnal travels when seeking revenge.

So it was the reaction against the cat's ancient 'holiness' in Egyptian religion, combined with the feline links with the Goddess Freya, and the cat's connection with childless isolated women, that made it the 'wicked' animal of the medieval period. Added to this was its haughtiness and its refusal to become completely subservient to human demands, unlike the dog, the horse, the sheep and other easily controlled domestic animals. Also, its nocturnal caterwauling during the breeding season gave rise to tales of orgies and secret feline ceremonies. The outcome was a savage persecution perpetuated against an animal whose only serious task was to rid human habitations of infestations of disease-carrying, food-spoiling rats and mice. It is a strange chapter in the history of Christian kindness.

3

FELINE FOLKTALES

'BELLING THE CAT'

The mice meet to discuss how to rid themselves of the cat. After a long debate they decide to tie a bell around the cat's neck, so that they can hear it approaching. The only difficulty is how to put the bell in place.

This ancient folktale is known from regions as widely separated as Estonia, Italy, Finland and the United States. The phrase 'belling the cat' is used to imply that an offered solution is impossible.

CAT CURES

In early centuries, cats were used in the making of certain potions and medicines. Perhaps because of their association with witches, it was thought that different parts of their bodies would have dramatic curative effects. In the seventeenth-century works of Edward Topsel, there are the following suggestions for the afflicted:

For gout: This can be cured by taking the fat of a cat 'and anointing therewith the sick part, and then wetting Wool or Tow in the same, and binding it to the offending place'.

For blindness: 'Take the head of a black Cat, which has not the spot of another colour in it and burn it to powder in an earthen pot leaded or glazed within, then take this powder and through a quill blow it thrice a day into thy eye…'

For gallstones: 'The liver of a Cat dryed and beat to powder is good against the stone.'

For fever: 'The dung of a female Cat with the claw of an Owl hanged about the neck of a man that hath had seven fits of Quartain Ague, cureth the same.'

For convulsion: 'a powder made of the gall of a black Cat... helpeth the convulsion and wryness of the mouth.'

For inducing the birth of a stillborn: '...if the gall of a Cat with the black dung of the same Cat, be burned in perfume under a woman travelling with a dead childe, it will cause it presently to come forth.'

In the Rev James Woodforde's *Diary of a Country Parson*, published in the eighteenth century, there is an additional feline cure:
For a stye on the eyelid: '...it is commonly said that the eyelid being rubbed by the tail of a black Cat, would do much good, if not entirely cure it.' (Having tried this himself with the tail of his own black tomcat, he reported that 'very soon after dinner I found my Eyelid much abated of the swelling and almost free from pain.')

Bibliography
1658. Topsel, E. *The History of Four-footed Beasts and Serpents*. London.

CAT'S PAW
A sixteenth-century fable in which a cunning monkey, wishing to take some roasted chestnuts out of a hot fire, does so by using the paw of a friendly cat. As a result, the term 'cat's paw' was applied to anyone who was a tool of another.

FABLES
Over the centuries many fables have been told that involve cats in one way or another. The earliest are those attributed to the Greek author Aesop, who is supposed to have lived in the sixth century BC.

It is not certain whether he actually existed, because it was several hundred years before 'Aesop's Fables' were collected together in written form. They appear to be an amalgam of ancient tales gathered from many sources. In the late seventeenth century, the French poet Jean de La Fontaine (1621–1695) adapted and amplified Aesop's Fables and published twelve books containing a total of 230 animal tales.

From these sources, examples of stories with a feline theme include the following:

The Cat and the Cock

The cat pounces on the cock and holds him tight, ready to kill and eat him. But first he feels he needs some excuse to do so. He decides that the terrible noise the cock makes every morning, disturbing the peace and quiet, is sufficient reason. But the cock argues that he is the world's alarm clock and that without him men will be late for their work. The cat listens to this reasonable defence but then ignores it and eats the cock anyway.

The Cat and the Fox

One day, the fox was explaining to the cat that it had a hundred different tricks with which it could survive. The cat replied that it had only one trick. Just then a pack of hounds appeared and the cat quickly climbed a tree, where it was safe. The fox went through its repertoire of one hundred tricks, one by one, but in the end was caught and killed by the hounds. (This story is well known all over Europe from Greece to Lapland.)

The Cat and the Hen

When the hen is ill the cat pays her a visit to ask if there is anything it can do to help. The hen replies that there is indeed something it can do, namely to go away and leave her in peace.

The Cat and the Mice

An old cat decides to use a trick to attract mice, so that it will not have to chase after them. It hangs itself upside-down from the wall, looking as though it is dead, and the mice start to come near. But a wise old mouse warns the younger ones to keep away, because a cat is not to be trusted, even it is stuffed with straw.

The Cat, the Weasel and the Rabbit

The rabbit and the weasel go to the elderly cat Raminagrobis to ask him to settle a dispute. They start to make their respective cases to him, but he complains of being deaf and asks them to come close enough for him to be able to hear what they are saying. When they do this, he lashes out at them, kills them, and settles their disagreement by eating them both.

The Eagle and the Cat

An eagle, a cat and a sow live together in a tree. The eagle has a nest for its young at the top of the tree. The sow and her piglets live at the foot of the tree. And the cat and her kittens live in a hollow half way up the trunk of the tree.

One day the cat tells the eagle that the sow is undermining the tree and it will collapse, and tells the sow that the eagle is about to attack her piglets and carry them off for food. Both the eagle and the sow are so terrified that they refuse to leave their young, even to look for food, and eventually all starve to death. The cat then feasts on their bodies.

Venus and the Cat

A female cat falls in love with a young man. Venus, the goddess of love, agrees to turn the cat into a beautiful girl. The young man marries the girl, but Venus wants to know whether her character has changed as well as her body and so she introduces a live mouse into the couple's bedroom. The girl instantly pounces on the mouse, much to her husband's dismay. Seeing this, Venus decides to turn the girl back into a cat again.

KIMONO CAT

According to Japanese folklore, a cat that is born with a special kind of black mark on its back is a spirit-bearing cat. If the shape of this black mark resembles a woman wearing a kimono, then the animal is believed to contain the spirit of one of the owner's ancestors. Should such a cat be born, it has to be carefully protected. It was common practice to send it to a temple for safekeeping, but occasionally one was stolen and removed from its native homeland.

It is known that such a theft took place at the beginning of the twentieth century, when a Chinese servant stole a Kimono Cat from a temple and smuggled her on to a ship bound for England. Her loss created a public scandal, but she reached London safely and went to live with a family in Putney. Called Kimona, she was well looked after and lived a suitably protected life until her death in 1911. A photograph of her reveals that she was a black and white cat with a black saddle marking on her back that could, with a little imagination, be interpreted as a fat lady wearing a kimono.

MAY KITTENS

There is a curious early European tradition that kittens born in the month of May should be destroyed, because if they are allowed to grow they will become 'dirty cats'. This bizarre idea is summed up in an old English proverb which baldly states: 'May chets bad luck begets, and sure to make dirty cats.'

The explanation reaches back into antiquity when, apparently, it was considered incorrect to indulge in sexual intercourse, or to marry, in this particular month. This was because people were supposed to be purifying themselves in readiness for the great midsummer celebrations in June.

PIOUS CAT

In fourteenth-century Persia, the poet Obaid-e Zakani wrote a children's story called *Mush u Gurba* (Cat and Mouse) that was to last for 600 years. It is still read by Iranian children today, but was little known in the West until Basil Bunting's delightful translation of it was published in 1986, under the title of *The Pious Cat*. Beneath the superficial simplicity of the children's fable lies a serious warning about the duplicity and tenacity of tyrants.

Briefly, the story tells how the devious cat Tibbald went to pray forgiveness for having killed and eaten a mouse. He offers a gift of compensation to every surviving relative of the mouse he has just eaten. The mice are delighted and they all flock see him, bringing him gifts. For their pains, he kills and eats all but two of them, who manage to escape. They run to the Mouse King, crying: 'Once on a time that ravenous ratter ate / his daily mouse at a steady flat rate, / but since he took to prayers and pieties, / he bolts us down in whole societies.' The Mouse King musters a huge army and war breaks out between the mice and the cats. Tibbald is caught and condemned to die on the gallows, but he manages to escape and swallows the Lord Chief Justice.

That is where the story ends, a salutary tale of the triumph of despots, and it is easy to see why it has retained its popularity, century after century, in a Middle East as infested by tyranny today as it was in Obaid-e Zakani's fourteenth century.

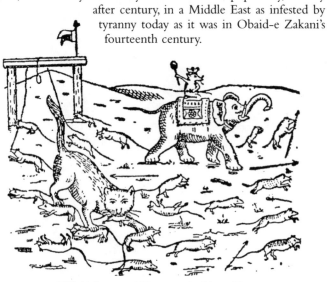

Tibbald the cat and his enemy the Mouse King

PUSS IN BOOTS

The story of The Master Cat, or Puss in Boots, in its present form, dates from the end of the seventeenth century. The French lawyer and author, Charles Perrault (1628–1703), who was a leading member of the Académie Française, wrote a number of tales to amuse his children, including 'Little Red Riding Hood', 'Cinderella', 'Sleeping Beauty' and 'Puss in Boots'. These were half-forgotten, traditional folktales of uncertain origin that he retold in a simple and attractive form and published as *Histoires et Contes du Temps Passé* or

Puss in Boots takes to the woods in search of prey

Contes de ma Mère l'Oie in 1697. They first appeared in English in 1729. There is a bronze statue of Perrault with Puss in Boots in the Tuileries gardens in Paris. The publication of the story, which depicts the cat, not as an evil creature, but as a clever animal, proved to be a major influence in changing and improving the cat's image in a Europe still bent on persecuting it as a witch's familiar and an embodiment of the Devil.

The simple story tells of a young man who is so poor that his cat is his only possession. He decides he has no choice but to eat the cat and wear its skin. The cat, however, persuades the young man that all will be well if only he will have a pair of boots made for him and give him a small pouch to carry. This is done and the cat takes to the woods where he snares a young rabbit and presents it to the king from the 'Marquis of Carabus', a name he has invented for his master. After Puss has pleased the king by taking him a number of gifts, he arranges a meeting between his master and the king's beautiful daughter. They fall in love and the king is delighted to give the couple his blessing because he believes the young man to be such a generous nobleman. The pair live happily ever after and Puss in Boots retires from his task of mouse catching and becomes a figure of great fame and importance.

This concept of a cat bringing his master good fortune undoubtedly influenced the development of the fanciful tale of Dick Whittington's Cat. Although Whittington was a real person, the story of his cat was a later fiction invented long after his death (see Chapter 10, Fictional Cats). Similar, early folktales of 'lucky cats' have been traced all over Europe, Africa, India, Indonesia and the West Indies.

A psychological analysis of the tale sees the cat as a symbol of man's native cunning – an intuitive cleverness that is used to gain success in life.

PUSSY WILLOW

There is an early Polish legend about the Pussy Willow that is found along river banks. It concerns a grey mother cat whose kittens were thrown into the river by a farmer who felt he already had enough cats to worry about. Their mother wept so loudly that the willows agreed to stretch themselves down into the water to rescue the drowning kittens. The kittens grabbed hold and were saved from a watery death. Ever since then, each spring, in memory of that event, the Pussy Willows grow soft grey furry buds which, to the touch, feel just like the fur of newborn kittens.

SUPERSTITIONS

There are more superstitions associated with cats than with any other animal, and the main ones are listed below.

Apart from a few that are concerned with a cat's reactions to alterations in the weather, where there may sometimes be an element of truth based on the cat's sensitivity to climatic changes, it is fair to say that they are all completely nonsensical. Many of them flatly contradict one another. However, they have been collected together here to show just how intense and widespread is the feeling that cats have some kind of supernatural influence. The superstitions have been grouped according to main topics, as follows:

Luck
1　Cats bring good luck.
2　Cats brings bad luck.
3　If a cat crosses the street it is a sign of bad luck.
4　If a black cat crosses your path, you will have good luck.
5　It is lucky to own a black cat, but unlucky to meet one.
6　Stroking a black cat brings good luck.
7　If a black cat is chased away it will take the luck of the house with it.
8　If a black cat pays you a brief visit it will bring you good luck.
9　If a black cat comes to stay it will bring you bad luck.
10　It is good luck to sleep with a cat.
11　Miners refuse to utter the word 'cat' when working down a mine.
12　Sailors refuse to say the word 'cat' at sea, although a ship's cat brings good luck.
13　If a sailor's wife keeps a cat it will ensure her husband's safe return.

14 At a theatre, a cat is good luck backstage.
15 If a theatre cat makes a mess backstage, the performance will be good.
16 Cats are bad luck on stage.
17 For a cricketer it is lucky to see a black cat when going out to bat.
18 A tortoiseshell cat brings luck to its owner.
19 A stray tortoiseshell coming into your home is an omen of misfortune.
20 A blue cat brings luck to its owner.
21 If your cat cries when you leave for a journey, some disaster will befall you.

A 'Spanish' or tortoiseshell cat, drawn in 1805

Health
22 It is bad for one's health to fondle cats.
23 If you kick a cat you will get rheumatism. ·
24 Cats suck the breath out of sleeping people.
25 Cats suffocate sleeping babies.
26 If your cat sneezes three times, everyone in the house will develop colds.
27 A wart can be cured by smearing three drops of cat's blood over it.
28 To get rid of warts, kill a cat and bury it in a black stocking.
29 Black cat broth cures consumption.
30 A stye on the eye can be cured by stroking it with a black cat's tail.
31 A dried cat's skin held to the face will cure toothache.
32 A cat' body boiled in olive oil makes a good dressing for wounds.
33 Water that has washed a sick person, if thrown over a cat, will cure that person if the cat is then driven from the house.

Weather

34 Cats can foretell the weather.

35 When a cat washes its face it is a sign of good weather.

36 When a cat washes its face it is a sign of rain.

37 If a cat looks out of the window it is looking for rain.

38 When a cat's pupil broadens there will be rain.

39 If a cat sneezes once, rain is coming.

40 Bathing a cat will bring rain.

41 A restless cat means a storm is brewing.

42 When a cat licks its tail a storm is coming.

43 If you throw a cat overboard there will be a storm at sea.

44 If you throw a cat overboard, you will raise a favourable wind.

45 If a ship's cat is playful, there will be a gale of wind astern.

46 If a ship's cat miaows on board ship, it will be a difficult voyage.

47 When a cat puts its tail towards the fire, bad weather is coming.

48 If a cat sits with its back to the fire there will be a frost.

49 If a cat claws the carpet there will be high winds.

50 If a cat dashes around the house, there will be high winds.

51 If a cat scratches the leg of a table there will be a change in the weather.

52 You can tell the tides by the pupils of a cat's eyes.

53 A kitten born in May will grow up melancholy.

Fertility

54 If the cat in your house is black, of lovers you will have no lack.

55 It is good luck to have the family cat at your wedding.

56 If a cat sneezes near a bride on her wedding morning, her happiness is assured.

57 A cat rocked in a cradle after a wedding will make a couple fertile.

58 A cat buried in a field of grain will help the crops to grow.

Visitors

59 When a cat washes its face company is coming.

60 If a cat washes itself in a doorway, a clergyman will visit the house.

Hunting

61 A kitten born in May will never be a mouser.

62 If you pay money for a cat it will never catch mice for you.

Spirits

63 The cat has psychic powers.

64 Cats can see ghosts.

65 A cat purrs when encountering a ghost.

66 If you take even one of the nine lives of a cat it will haunt you.

67 A black cat is the Devil.

68 If you drown a cat the Devil will get you.

69 If a black cat crosses your path, Satan has been taking notice of you.

70 Witches can change themselves into cats.

71 A black cat is a witch's familiar.

72 When a holy man dies his spirit will enter a cat; when the cat dies his spirit is free.

73 A cat has nine lives.

Death

74 Cats prey on corpses.

75 If a cat jumps over a corpse, that corpse will become a vampire.

76 If a cat leaves the house of an invalid and cannot be coaxed back he will die.

77 If a sick person dreams of cats he will die.

78 If a sick person sees two cats fighting he will die.

79 If there is a corpse indoors, a cat will desert the house.

80 A dying cat will attract Death to the house.

4

LEGENDARY CATS

ABUHERRIRA'S CAT

A pet belonging to one of the companions of the prophet Mohammed, Abu Huraira. Such was his love of cats that he was known as 'the father of the little cat'. In Goethe's poem 'The Favoured Beasts', his favourite cat was one of the four animals admitted to the Moslem paradise: 'Abuherrira's Cat, too, here purrs around his master blest, for holy must the beast appear the Prophet has caressed'.

AELWAER'S CAT

Saint Aelwaer was a satirical image meant to display attributes that were the exact opposite of the qualities of the Virgin Mary. She was described as a 'demonic anti-saint, patroness of all tribulation… an intemperate cavalier, mother of all vices…a sort of Virgin Mary in reverse.' In a Dutch woodcut of 1550 she is portrayed riding a donkey, with a magpie on her head symbolizing immorality, a pig under her left arm symbolizing gluttony, and a cat held aloft on her right hand symbolizing the forces of evil. The cat is raised high like an emblem or ensign and is clearly meant to advertise the fact that this figure is in league with the Devil, for this was the period when Europe was brutally persecuting all felines as familiars of witches and creatures of wickedness.

BASTET

Bastet was a sacred cat goddess of ancient Egypt. Her name means literally 'She of the City of Bast'.

Cats had played several roles in the ancient civilization of Egypt, and had been domesticated for many centuries before the cult of the friendly, protective goddess Bastet started to grow and flourish. An earlier feline goddess had been far from friendly. She was a fierce, lion-headed, war goddess called Sekhmet. Bloodthirsty and terrifying, she bore no relation to the increasingly important, small domesticated cat that was ridding Egypt of its detested rodent pests. With the rise of this valued companion cat, something had to change. A new, more helpful goddess was needed. Around 1500BC, this began to happen. Sekhmet was joined by the new goddess Bastet and they were seen as a contrasting pair. Together they represented the two faces of the sun: Sekhmet was the cruel, searing heat of the destructive sun, while Bastet was the warming, life-giving aspect.

As the domestic cat became more and more respected (and the threat of attack from wild lions became less and less likely), Bastet gradually began to dominate as the major feline deity. The Egyptians cleverly explained away this shift of emphasis in a legendary tale, recorded on an ancient papyrus. The goddess 'had fled in a temper to the Nubian desert where she hid in the shape of a lioness. Her father, who needed her presence to protect him against his enemies, sent Onuris and Thoth to bring her back to Egypt. The messengers of the Sun managed to persuade her to return. On the way home she drowned her anger by bathing in the sacred waters of Philae on the southern border of Egypt, calmly adopting the form of a cat. She sailed down the Nile acclaimed by the people on the banks, until she came to Bubastis, which became a holy place where periodic feasts were held in her honour.'

This story neatly converted the angry old lion goddess into a friendly new cat goddess, and the Cult of the Cat was under way. Bubastis, a town about 60 kilometres (37 miles) north-east of Cairo, became the headquarters of this cult and a huge temple was built there to honour Bastet. (Sadly, little of this red granite temple survives today.)

At first, Bastet was only a local deity, but her fame spread until she was known and revered far and wide. Each year vast crowds descended on the town for the annual celebrations. These became the most popular, the bawdiest and the most drunken in all of Egypt. Writing in the fifth century BC, Herodotus reported that, as the crowds converged on Bubastis: 'men and women embark together, and great numbers of both sexes in every barge.' They made music, playing castanets and flutes and clapping their hands to the sound. Whenever they came near to a town, on their way to the festival, they would stop the barge and 'shout and scoff at the women of the place; some dance, others stand up and pull up their clothes; this they do at every town by the riverside'. This hint at ribald sexual exposure reflects the fecundity aspect of the cat goddess.

It is thought that the main attraction of Bastet's religious festivals was that they were essentially an excuse for drunken, mass orgies. According to Herodotus, 'more wine is consumed at this festival than in all the rest of the year' and this appealing form of religious ceremony attracted men and women: 'to the number of seven hundred thousand.'

Although this figure is undoubtedly a wild exaggeration, it is clear that Bastet was by far the most popular deity ever known in ancient Egypt, and it is not surprising that literally thousands of small bronze images of her, in the shape of a sitting cat, were found amongst the rubble of the temple ruins. Apart from offering Bastet small bronze effigies of herself, people also took mummified cats to the festivals to gain favour with the goddess by showing their reverence for their dead feline pets. (For more information on cat mummies, see Chapter 2, Feline History.) This clearly illustrates one of the dangers of becoming a symbolic animal: you end up as more of a revered abstract generality than a much loved individual pet.

The cult of Bastet lasted for over a thousand years, during which time she offered an impressive range of protections to her followers, including protection in childbirth, against illness, against infertility, and against all bodily dangers, especially from poisonous animals. She protected children, especially the newborn, and she was also the goddess of pleasure, music and dance. With these valuable qualities it is hardly surprising that her popularity was so great. However it was doubtless this role in licentious celebration that led to so much misery for cats in later centuries at the hands of pious, tight-lipped

Christians. The idea that sacred ceremonies could be fun was soon to be crushed by a miserable new puritanism, and suppressed forever.

Alternative names for Bastet are Bast, Pasht, or Ubasti.

Butter Cat

In Scandinavia there was a mythical cat known over a wide range as the 'Butter Cat'. Unlike most legendary cats, this one was not evil, but a protector and a provider. Because it was noticed that cats loved cream, it became a superstitious belief that they were 'bringers of gifts', especially milk and butter. In Finland this benign cat was known as 'Para'. Further north, in Lapland, she became 'Smieragatto'.

Cactus Cat

The Cactus Cat was one of the 'fearsome critters' invented in the nineteenth century by the frontiersmen of the American West. It was an amusement of theirs to pass the time telling tall tales and these developed into a whole cycle of bizarre animals. The Cactus Cat had thorny hair, especially exaggerated on the ears. Its tail was branched. On its front legs there were savage, sharp blades of bone, with which it slashed the giant cacti to get at the sap within. The sap fermented and the cat then drank it, quickly becoming intoxicated, after which it ran off uttering horrible screams.

Cait Sith

According to the folklore of the Scottish Highlands, there exists a fairy cat called the Cait Sith. It is larger than a domestic cat, black in colour and with a white spot on its breast. It has an arched back and erect bristles in its fur. Unlike other fairy creatures, this one is believed to have a solid physical presence. It is thought to be a transformed witch. In reality, the Cait Sith is almost certainly what is now known as the Kellas Cat – a large black hybrid between feral domestic cats and Scottish wild cats. Specimens of these impressive hybrids were examined scientifically in the 1980s.

Bibliography
1989. Shuker, K. *Mystery Cats of the World*. Robert Hale, London.

CAT-A-MOUNTAIN

Marco Polo reported the existence of a predatory cat in the Far East with the body of a leopard but with a strange skin that stretches out when it hunts, enabling it to fly in pursuit of its prey. The Cat-a-Mountain appears to be an imaginative amalgam of a big cat and a large bat, but later authors frequently used it simply as a name for a wild cat. By the seventeenth century some authors had abbreviated it to Catamount .

CCOA

Ccoa is an evil cat demon, greatly feared by the South American Indians of the Quechua tribe in Peru. He is about 1m (3ft) long, with dark stripes down the length of his body. He has a large head with glowing eyes. He controls hail and lightning, with which he sets out to ruin crops and destroy people. He has to be appeased by regular offerings, to prevent him from causing havoc.

CURLY LEGGED CAT

Within the pages of the vast, thirteen-volume, seventeenth-century *Natural History of Aldrovandus*, there lurks a bizarre feline, the Curly legged Cat. It appears to be a striped tabby cat with both its right front and right rear legs curled around in a spiral. The author's only comment on this strange creature is that it was so afflicted from birth. It was either a freak mutation (that must have kept falling on its side) or, more likely, was a garbled interpretation of a crippled cat that had at some time in the past been run over by a coach wheel.

Bibliography
1638–1668. Aldrovandus. *Opera Omnia*.
1890. Ashton, J. *Curious Creatures in Zoology*. Nimmo, London.

Illustration of the curly legged cat from Aldrovandus.

EGYPTIAN CATS

Few people are unaware that the cat was important to the ancient Egyptians, but there is often confusion about its precise role. This is because it did, in fact, have several quite distinct roles. Writing in 1990, Jason Morris separated out five major categories, based on depictions in the art of ancient Egypt, as follows:

1 The cat as household companion

In about a dozen cases, the cat is depicted as a small, domesticated animal positioned beneath the chair of its owners. Amazingly, although these pictures are very similar to one another in design, they span nearly 800 years and nine dynasties (roughly from 2000 to 1200BC). In each case, the cat is shown in close proximity to its female owner, usually under her own chair. This either means that cats were the pets of Egyptian women, rather than men, or that the close juxtaposition had some special, perhaps sexual significance.

In several cases, these household cats are shown performing a naturalistic activity. One of them strains at its leash as it tries to get at a bowl of food; another devours a fish on the floor, perhaps sharing in a banquet; a third sits apprehensively still on its owner's barge as it glides along; another strikes out at a bird with its paw; another has its mouth open and its tongue hanging out, as if it is overheating at a banquet; another is holding a duck while a pet monkey leaps over its head; another gnaws at a bone held in its paw; another shows a cat striking out at a threatening goose. These natural actions contrast with the highly traditional positioning of the cat beneath the chair in each case. They clearly show that these were lively, real cats, taking part in the everyday life of the household. Several of them wearing some kind of decorative collars, suggesting that they were special pet cats rather than mere working mousers.

2 The cat as hunting companion

Only the Egyptians, who were amazingly adept at domesticating a whole range of animal species, attempted to use the cat as a hunting companion. Everywhere else in the world, this role was reserved for the dog, but Egyptian art shows with great clarity and detail the way

Nebamun's cat hunting birds in the marches, 1450BC

in which owners took their cats with them on hunting trips in the marshlands of the Nile, when in pursuit of fish or birds.

There are several such scenes dating from 1880 to 1450BC. One shows a cat hunting birds while its master spears fish from his barge; another shows a cat on a barge pawing impatiently at its master's clothes, as the man hurls a throwing-stick at a cluster of birds on the shore; another shows a cat flushing out game for its master; another shows a cat in the midst of a cluster of startled birds, snatching and grabbing at them as best it can, while its master, on a barge, is in the act of hurling a throwing stick.

3   The cat as humorous figure

Roughly between 1300 and 1000BC, there are a number of humorous cats, depicted almost in the style of modern cartoon cats. They show the cat in various satirical roles, probably illustrating well-known legends and stories of the day. Among these, there is one in which mice are shown besieging a fortress defended unsuccessfully by cats; in another, there is a duel between a cat and a mouse, presided over by an eagle; in another, cats are shown dancing attendance on an enthroned mouse and bringing her gifts; in another, cats assist at the toilet of a Queen Mouse; and in yet another, mice bring food and drink to a cat to bargain for peace; others show cats driving flocks of geese.

4   The cat as serpent slayer

In the New Kingdom Period (roughly 1500–1000BC) the great Sun God, Re, is often depicted as a cat attacking the evil serpent of darkness, Apopis, and slicing off its head. This symbolizes the battle between darkness and light. If the cat does not succeed, the sun will not rise again and darkness will cover the land forever. There are at least four well-known depictions of this struggle, each showing the cat wielding a pointed knife and with the serpent heaving its coils into the air. The knife is in the act of severing the snake's head.

5   The cat as a goddess

From roughly 1500 to 30BC, the cat in Egypt became sacred. As the goddess Bastet, she was worshipped in great temples, mummified by the million and endlessly modelled in bronze. (For further information on Bastet, see earlier in this chapter.)

Bibliography

1940. Langton, N & Langton, B. *The Cat in Ancient Egypt*. Cambridge University Press.

1990. Morris, J. *The Cat in Ancient Egypt*. Unpublished Thesis, Ashmolean Museum.

1993. Malek, J. *The Cat in Ancient Egypt*. British Museum, London.

FREYA'S CATS

The great chariot of the blue-eyed, blonde goddess Freya was drawn through the heavens by a pair of magnificent cats. These legendary felines symbolized the twin qualities of their Scandinavian mistress, namely fecundity and ferocity. Like real cats they were normally affectionate and loving, but fierce if roused.

Freya (or Freyja) was originally the Viking Goddess of sex, love and fertility. She wept golden tears and roamed the night skies in the form of a she goat. She wore a special necklace, a symbol of her sexuality, which she obtained by sleeping with each of the four dwarves who fashioned it. She was the patroness of a witchcraft cult that involved trances, foretelling the future, and the performance of orgiastic rites.

In fifteenth-century Germany the cult of Freya enjoyed a revival that was ultimately to cause thousands of innocent cats untold pain and misery. Because of the ancient association between Freya and her felines, the German followers of her cult used to round up as many cats as possible and forcibly introduce them into the ceremonies at their wild nocturnal orgies. Not surprisingly, this led to a powerful connection, in the popular mind, between cats and witchcraft. Then, when Pope Innocent VIII formally condemned the followers of Freya, the unfortunate cats were caught in the same net. In his edict of 1484 he declared that all women who worshipped Freya should be burned at the stake. And he added that their cats should be burned with them.

The Viking goddess Freya and her magnificent cat riding through the skies

According to one source, the holocaust that followed led to the deaths by fire of 10 per cent of the entire female population of Germany. Inevitably, it also led to the torture and killing of a vast number of cats. This nightmare phase of feline history persisted through the sixteenth, seventeenth and eighteenth centuries, the onslaught spreading out from Germany across the whole of Europe and even to the New World. It did not die out until the nineteenth century, when, at last, Victorian England began to take a more enlightened attitude towards animal life.

GOLDEN FLOWER

In Japan it was red cats, rather than black ones, that used to be feared for their magical powers. Known as 'Golden Flowers' (*kinkwa-neko*), they were thought to be able to transform themselves into beautiful women. Although this might appear to be an improvement on 'ugly old witches', the alluring form that these supernatural cats took made them even more dangerous. In a famous legend, one of these glamorous cat women causes the downfall of a powerful feudal lord.

KILKENNY CATS

The expression 'to fight like Kilkenny Cats' means to fight to the bitter end. It stems from a legend about two cats tortured by soldiers in eighteenth-century Ireland. The soldiers were supposed to have tied two cats together by their tails and hung them over a line to watch them fight to the death. However, one soldier decided to release them. He could only do this by cutting off their tails, whereupon the tailless cats immediately fled. The soldier was still holding their severed tails when an officer arrived and asked what had happened. The soldier invented the story that two cats had been fighting savagely and had devoured each other except for their tails.

KING OF CATS

In an old Irish legend there is a huge cat, the King of Cats, who ruled over all the other cats. His name was Irusan and he lived in a cave at Knowth. His end came when, learning that a poet had made satirical remarks about cats, he carried the poet off and, as he did so, was killed by a saint who drove a red hot bar through his body.

There is an old Irish folktale that makes reference to the importance of the King of Cats to other felines: a man was killing a cat but before it died it told him to go home and say he had just killed the King of Cats... This he did, but when his own pet cat heard the news, it leapt up from its resting place by the side of the fire and tore him to pieces.

MATAGOT

The Matagot is a good luck cat. Any family sheltering, feeding and caring for such an animal will attract immense wealth to their house. The Matagot is always a black cat and it has strange, magical powers.

The name is used in the south of France, where there is a special formula for becoming rich with the aid of this 'magician cat'. Because the Matagot is greedy, you must lure him with a plump chicken. Once you have hold of his tail you must put him into a sack and, without once looking back over your shoulder, you must secretly take him to your home. When you arrive there, you must place him in a large chest and make sure to offer him the first mouthful of every meal you have. If you do all this, you will find a gold coin deposited next to the chest each morning.

This belief was especially strong near Marseilles, where a nickname for the Matagot was 'Coste'. To this day, according to Fernand Mery, there are still people living in Provence with the surname of Coste-Matagot. In Brittany the Matagot is known as the *chat d'argent*, a black cat that can serve nine masters at once (presumably with its nine lives) and make them all rich.

This legend of a cat that can bring riches to its owner is found in the folklore of many countries, including Denmark, Italy and Iran. In England it was the basis of the legend of Dick Whittington and his cat.

PATRIPATAN

A white cat called Patripatan was dispatched by his princely master to pluck a flower from a tree in heaven. The cat found heaven so enchanting that the days and weeks flew by. After 300 years had passed, Patripatan remembered his task and knew he must return. He had been such pleasant company that the gods gave him, not just a single flower, but a whole flowering branch of the wonderful tree, to take back with him to Salangham, his home in India. While he had been away his prince and the people of Salangham had not aged at all and, on the cat's return, their country became a land of serenity and beauty.

RE

In ancient Egypt, during the New Kingdom (1567–1085BC), the great Sun God Re (or Ra) took the form of a cat every night to do battle with the powers of darkness in the shape of a gigantic serpent, called Apopis. Every night Apopis would lie in wait for Re, hoping to attack and kill him and thus prevent the sun from rising. And every night, the great cat Re had to defeat the snake. He managed this every time, and the sun rose again, but on very rare occasions he suffered a serious temporary defeat, causing an eclipse.

The battle between the cat and the snake is depicted a number of times in the art of ancient Egypt, and for 500 years follows essentially the same pattern. The cat Re is shown squatting on his haunches, holding a sharp, pointed knife with a curiously tapered blade in one of its front paws. With this weapon he is seen in the act of decapitating the fiendish serpent of darkness. The body of the serpent is always shown thrown up into vertical coils, as if writhing from the savage attack. Despite these nightly decapitations, Apopis somehow manages to keep his head for the next assault, and the confrontation goes on, night after night, for eternity.

The cat itself is shown either as a mackerel-striped tabby, or as a spotted cat, or as a dark, plain cat with a white ruff, face and paws. This last variant suggests that the model in that instance was a Jungle Cat (*Felis chaus*), rather than the usual domestic cat.

Among popular writers, the Sun God is usually referred to as Ra, but Egyptologists prefer the spelling Re.

SINH

According to legend, Sinh was the founding father of the Birman breed, the sacred cat of Burma. Sinh belonged to the high priest, Mun-Ha, and was with the old man when he died during an attack on his ancient Burmese temple. Placing his paws on the body of the dying man, Sinh absorbed the soul of the priest and, as he did so, his paws turned white.

VAMPIRE CAT

In ancient Japanese folklore, the Vampire Cat of Nabéshima plays a role very similar to that of the Vampire Bat in Western mythology. The demon cat kills a beautiful maiden by biting her neck and sucking out her blood. It then buries her body and assumes her identity. In its new female form, it then turns its attention to the maiden's lover, a handsome prince. By gradually extracting the prince's life force from his body, during nightly visits, the vampire weakens him almost to the point of death. The prince's aide, concerned about his master's condition, decides to stand guard over him throughout the night, and eventually forces the demonic cat to flee the palace. It escapes to the mountains where it is finally hunted down and killed.

As recently as 1929, a report in a London newspaper suggested that this dreaded vampire cat was once again active and was, according to local belief in Japan, setting out to ensnare the wives of descendants of the old Samurai warriors.

There is also a Spanish-Jewish folktale about a vampire cat. According to this legend, Lilith was the first wife of Adam, but left him and flew away as a vampire. She became immortal and took the shape of a huge black cat called El Broosha. In this form, she descends in the night on innocent, sleeping babies and sucks the blood out of them. Author Mildred Kirk has suggested that this might be the origin of the completely false idea that pet cats should not be allowed in the same room as a sleeping baby, because they may sit on the child and suffocate it.

WHITE CAT

According to some authorities, the legend of the White Cat is based on an early fable that originated with Aesop. In this tale, Venus agrees to turn a beautiful White Cat into a princess, so that she can be united with the handsome young man she loves. The princess manages to hide her true identity from her beloved until she happens to see a rat scampering across the bedroom floor. At that moment she cannot resist the temptation to leap out of bed and chase after the rodent, thus giving the game away.

This tale is not, however, the traditional fairy-story that is usually associated with 'The Legend of the White Cat'. For that we must turn to France where, in 1682, the Comtesse D'Aulnoy wrote a fairytale, using that title, in which a young prince falls in love with a beautiful white cat and wants to marry her. She tells him he must cut off her head and her tail and throw them in the fire, which, with great reluctance, he does. At this, she is freed from an ancient curse and is turned back into the beautiful princess she once was. The prince is overjoyed and they live happily ever after.

Although once immensely popular, this folktale has lost ground in the twentieth century, being almost completely overshadowed by the stories of Dick Whittington and his Cat and Puss in Boots.

Bibliography

1803. *The Renowned History of the White Cat*. Harris, London.
1847. *The White Cat*. Blackwood, Edinburgh.
1863. *The History of the White Cat*. Routledge, London.
1867. *The White Cat*. Nimmo, Edinburgh.
1870. *The White Cat*. McLoughlin, New York.
1873. *The White Cat*. Gall & Inglis, Edinburgh.
1893. *The White Cat*. Farqharson, London.
1905. *The White Cat*. Altemus, Philadelphia.
1906. *The White Cat*. Newnes, London.
1914. *The White Cat*. Arnold, London
1923. *The White Cat*. Blackie, London.
1925. *Tales of the Fairies; The White Cat*. Chelsea, London.
1955. *Columbine the White Cat*. Concora, New York.

The prince cuts off the beautiful White Cat's head and tail

5

FAMOUS CAT OWNERS

AILUROPHILIA IS the technical term for the love of cats. Many famous people, especially authors, can be classified as genuine ailurophiles. Some famous figures become cat lovers only by association, but most of the celebrated names listed below have a genuine history of devotion to felines.

BRIAN ALDISS

The renowned poet, playwright, critic, fiction and science-fiction writer (1925–) has enjoyed the company of a number of cats: Macramé, Yum-Yum, Foxie, Jackson and Nickie. 'At many human faults a cat will never take offence; Two things though they cannot stand: The wretched Door, the horrid Fence.'

KINGSLEY AMIS

Like many authors who must spend long hours at their keyboard, Kingsley Amis (1922–1995) enjoyed the company of a cat. In his case it was a magnificent, long-haired, green-eyed, pure white cat called Sarah Snow. He referred to her as a 'Hertfordshire White', but she looked remarkably like an old-fashioned Angora.

Like many cat owners, he had strong reservations about people who do not have house-pets: 'I am enough of a cat-lover to be suspicious of a household that doesn't have a cat... I associate a person having a cat with them being gentler than other people.'

He admitted to talking to his cat. 'People are silly about their cats… There is no point in having a cat and being prosaic about it. Cats stimulate the fancy; we weave fantasies about them.'

His own fantasy about Sarah Snow was that she was trying to learn English. In his 1987 poem 'Cat-English', he comments:

'If you've a sympathetic ear, Cat-English comes through loud
and clear,
Of course, the words are short and few, the accent strange and
strident, too,
And our side never gets a crack, at any sort of answer back.'

Bibliography
1988. Surges, M. *The English Cat at Home*. Chatto and Windus, London.

BRIGITTE BARDOT
When she retired from film-making, the French actress Brigitte Bardot devoted herself to animal welfare. In 1986 she established the Bardot Foundation in St Tropez. The following year she sold her jewellery and other personal possessions to raise the funds necessary for her welfare work. In her own home she gives shelter to sixty neutered stray cats that are allowed to sleep with her at night.

CHARLES BAUDELAIRE
The French poet's obsession with cats was so great that he frequently caused minor scandals on occasions when he paid more attention to the animals than to his human companions. Even his friends referred to his reactions to cats as 'startling and excessive', and he was ridiculed in the press. One journalist complained:

'It has become the fashion in the society formed by Baudelaire and his companions to make too much of cats… Baudelaire, going for the first time to a house, and on business, is uneasy and restless until he has seen the household cat.

But when he sees it he takes it up, kisses and strokes it, and is so completely occupied with it that he makes no answer to anything that is said to him. People stare at this breach of good manners, but he is a man of letters, an oddity, and the lady of the house henceforth regards him with curiosity.'

So great was the poet's affinity for cats that he himself was once described as being 'a voluptuous wheedling cat, with velvety manners'.

ALEXANDER BORODIN

The Russian composer Borodin (1833–1887) and his wife passed their days surrounded by cats. Rimsky-Korsakov's bemused account of their tolerance of their feline companions includes the following observations.

The cats 'paraded across the dinner-table, sticking their noses into plates, unceremoniously leaping to the diner's back...You might sit at their tea-table – and behold! Tommy marches along the board and makes for your plate. You shoo him off, but [Mrs Borodin] invariably takes his part... Meanwhile, zip! another cat has bounded at [Borodin's] neck and, twining himself about it, has fallen to warming that neck without pity.'

One of their tabby cats was called Rybolov, meaning Fisherman, because he managed to catch small fish through the ice-holes. Another tabby was named Dlinyenki, meaning 'Longy'. According to Rimsky-Korsakov, he was in the habit of bringing home kittens by the scruff of the neck. If he was indeed a 'he', this is remarkable behaviour, but the chances are that the great composer was mistaken and that 'he' was really a 'she' who was simply bringing her kittens home to the security of the house.

CHU HOU-TSUNG

The Emperor of China, Chu Hou-Tsung (1507–1566), the eleventh Emperor of the Ming Dynasty, had a favourite cat called Shuang-mei, which translates as 'Frost-eyebrows'. According to a contemporary report: 'She was of faintly blue colour but her two eyebrows were clearly jade-white... wherever her Imperial master went, she always led. She waited upon the Emperor until he slept and then she lay still like a stump.'

When she died she was given a special honour, being buried in a grave with a stone tablet inscribed with the words 'Ch'iu-lung Chung'. This means 'The Grave of a Dragon with Two Horns',

A Chinese cat, by the artist Chu Lin

which was a term of special praise when applied to a person and therefore even more flattering when applied to a cat.

WINSTON CHURCHILL

The wartime prime minister adored cats and never failed to react to their presence, even at the height of the war. Both in the Cabinet Room and Churchill's dining room, a chair next to him was reserved for his favourite cat. The main occupant of these chairs was a black cat from Admiralty House appropriately named Nelson. This cat, which, from 1940, also shared the great man's bed, was helping the war effort, said Churchill, by acting as a hot water bottle and therefore saving fuel.

Among his various cats were Bob, a black and white cat who waited for the PM at the steps of No. 10 Downing Street and was usually rewarded with a friendly stroking; Mr Cat (also known as Mr Kat or Tango), with whom he discussed political issues; the autocratic Nelson; an adopted stray called Margate; and Jock, a ginger tom given to him on his 88th birthday by Sir John Colville, and who was mentioned in Churchill's will.

COLETTE

French novelist (1873–1954) with a lifelong passion for cats, who wrote a number of well-known books about her pets. She is quoted as saying: 'Making friends with a cat can only be a profitable experience.'

Bibliography

1913. *Barks and Purrs*. Fitzgerald, New York. (= *Sept dialogues de betes*) About her grey Angora Cat, Kiki-la-Doucette and its companion, a French bulldog called Toby.

1924. *Cats, Dogs and I*. Holt, New York. (= stories from *La paix chez les bêtes*)

1936. *The Cat*. Farrar and Rinehart, New York. (= *La Chatte*) About a cat called Saha, a blue-grey Chartreux, whose owner left his wife because she was cruel to the animal.

1951. *Creatures Great and Small*. Secker and Warburg, London. (= *Dialogues des bêtes*; *Sept dialogues des bêtes*; *Douze dialogues des bêtes*; *La paix chez les bêtes*).

1953. *Gigi and the Cat*. Secker and Warburg, London. (= new translation of *La Chatte*).

ANNE FRANK

Three cats, Tommy, Boche and Mouschi, were the wartime companions of Anne Frank, the German Jewish girl who, with the posthumous publication of her *Diary of a Young Girl* in 1947, became a symbol of Jewish suffering during World War II. Having fled with her family to Amsterdam to escape Nazi persecution, the thirteen-year-old girl was forced to go into hiding in a warehouse attic in 1942. She and her family shared their secret hiding place with the cats for three years before being betrayed by informers. When she first arrived at her hiding place she found two of the cats already there. One was an aggressive warehouse cat that was always the first to attack, so she called it Boche. The other, an attic cat, was repeatedly forced to retaliate, but always won in the end, so she called it Tommy. The third was Mouschi, the pet of the fifteen-year-old son of some family friends, who eventually joined the Franks in hiding.

THÉOPHILE GAUTIER

The French Romantic author Théophile Gautier (1811–1872) was a fanatical cat lover who shared his life with a succession of unusual cats. In his book *La Ménagerie Intime* he describes some of them as follows:

1   Childebrand was a splendid gutter-cat, striped black and tan... with a distant tigerish look.

2   Madame-Théophile was a red and white cat who stole food from the author when morsels were 'on their way from my plate to my mouth'.

3   Don Pierrot de Navarre was an immaculate white cat that watched the author's pen closely as he wrote, and 'would snatch the pen out of my hand' as if to take over the writing himself.

4   Séraphita, another pure white cat, was dreamy, reserved, luxuriating and addicted to perfume.

5,6,7   Don Pierrot and Séraphita produced three jet black kittens called Enjoras, Gavroche and Eponine, named after characters in Victor Hugo's *Les Misérables*. Eponine regularly dined at table with her master.

8   Zizi was a magnificent angora who enjoyed making music by walking up and down the keyboard of Gautier's piano.

9   Cléopatre was Eponine's daughter, a tawny-black cat that liked to stand on three legs, 'her fourth lifted up like a classical lion that has lost its marble ball'.

Gautier is said to have loved cats so passionately that, at times, 'he cared for nothing else', and his writings about them clearly reveal the extent of his obsession.

An illustration from Gautier's La Menagerie Intime

GREGORY THE GREAT

St Gregory the Great (540–604) – Pope Gregory I – was a man whose mildness, tolerance and joy in pastoral simplicity were completely out of character with the epoch in which he lived. Originally a Roman civil servant, he so hated the chaos of his world that he retired into a monastery where he spent what he described as the happiest days of his life. When he emerged three years later he was eventually to rise to the highest office in the church, but in the peace of the monastery he lived a quiet, serene existence with a feline companion. His biographer, Jacobus Diaconus, records that 'he possessed nothing in the world except a cat, which he carried in his bosom, frequently caressing it, as his sole companion.'

That is the official story, but it seems that, over the centuries, it has suffered considerably in the re-telling. In an alternative version, which may be closer to the truth, it is recorded that a hermit, whose only possession was a cat, was told in a dream that he would 'be in the same place as Pope Gregory'. He was unhappy about this because he did not want to be associated with such a wealthy man as the Pope. But then he had another dream in which the Lord ticked him off for being so proud of his poverty: 'Since a man is not rich by reason of what he owns, but of what he loves, how dare you compare your poverty with Gregory's wealth, when you can be convicted of showing more affection for that cat of yours, fondling it every day and sharing it with no one, than he does for all his riches, which he does not love, but lavishes on all?'

If the story of the hermit is true, then it would seem that Pope Gregory was a cat lover and cat owner, not in person, but only by association with an ailurophilic hermit who spiritually identified himself with the great man.

THOMAS HARDY

The great English novelist, Thomas Hardy (1840–1928) was so passionate about his pet cat that, when it died, he buried it under a small mound beneath its favourite tree and composed a long obituary poem to it, declaring: 'Never another pet for me! Let your place all vacant be...'

He was good to his word, refusing to have another for many years until, as an old man, he was given a grey Persian Cat with deep orange eyes called Cobby that he could not resist. He adored Cobby and the cat stayed loyally by his side until he died, when it vanished without trace.

An intriguing explanation of Cobby's strange disappearance has recently been provided by author Frank Smyth. If true, it must surely rank as one of the oddest tales of a pet cat's relationship with its owner. It seems that, when Hardy died, a conflict arose concerning where his body should rest. For the nation, it had to lie in Poets'

Corner at Westminster Abbey, but since, during his life, he had given his heart (metaphorically) to the village of Stinsford, near Dorchester, it was decided that, in death, his heart would (literally) be given to that village. Two small bronze urns were prepared, one to contain his ashes for the Abbey and the other to hold his heart, to be buried in a grave at St Michael's Church in the village. A doctor was called in and quickly removed the heart, which was indeed buried, with appropriate formalities, in the graveyard. The tombstone can be seen there to this day, proclaiming 'Here Lies the Heart of Thomas Hardy'. But matters were not quite as simple as they seemed.

What actually occurred, according to Frank Smyth, is that the heart was removed from Hardy's body while his corpse was still lying in his house. It was carefully wrapped in a tea towel and the towel was then placed in a biscuit tin. The tin was left beside the body. Cobby the cat had loved to stay close to the old man during his final days, and probably expected to be fed there. So he can hardly be blamed if, sniffing what appeared to be a tin full of meat, he did his best to open it. He must have been puzzled by the old man's refusal to help him, but he struggled on and eventually managed to remove the lid. Inside was a new kind of cat food, but he ate it up greedily, having no doubt been somewhat neglected in all the drama surrounding the great author's demise. All he left uneaten were a few valves and gristly bits.

The next day, the undertaker arrived to collect the heart for burial. All he found were an open biscuit tin, a few scraps of heart and a plump, contented cat. It was his solemn duty to bury Hardy's heart in the village graveyard and so it was clear to him what he must do. Without a moment's hesitation, he quickly strangled the cat, put it inside the biscuit tin and then proceeded as planned, as though nothing unusual had happened.

The only strange feature of the subsequent church ceremony was that, standing before the altar in the church, in place of the small bronze urn that had been promised, there was a 'polished wooden box, about the size and shape of a biscuit tin'. No explanation was given for this last-minute change, the service took place normally and the box was duly laid to rest, containing Hardy's heart as formally required. However, the congregation was spared the news that the revered organ was nestling, not in a neatly wrapped funeral cloth, but instead inside the stomach of his much loved pet cat, old Cobby, an animal of whom it truly could be said, he stole the old man's heart in more ways than one.

When archaeologists come to explore Hardy's tomb a thousand years from now, they will doubtless reach the conclusion that the skeleton of a cat found there proves conclusively that the famous novelist (who was in reality a down-to-earth atheist) wished to have his beloved cat accompany him to the afterlife.

ERNEST HEMINGWAY

The tough, outdoor, huntsman, man-of-action image created by American author Ernest Hemingway (1898–1961), is strangely at odds with his private love of cats. At home, one would expect to see him accompanied by faithful, subservient gundogs and hounds, but instead he is found surrounded by a whole colony of pampered felines. He wrote *For Whom the Bell Tolls* at a desk covered in cats.

The Hemingway house, on a hilltop in Havana, was overrun with no fewer than thirty pet cats and such was the chaos that his wife Mary insisted on building them a separate 'White Tower', complete with special feeding, sleeping and maternity facilities. Even after it was completed, several of the cats, including Crazy Christian, Friendless Brother and Ecstasy, were soon back in the main house with their besotted master. It is reported that, when he was working on *A Farewell to Arms*, the cat-count had risen to thirty-four. At one stage he began crossing local Cuban cats with Angoras in an attempt to create a new Hemingway breed.

The author had such trust in his cats that, in earlier days when living in Paris, he and his wife allowed their yellow-eyed cat called 'F. Puss' to babysit for them. Friends were horrified because they were convinced that the cat would lie on the baby and suffocate it. Needless to say, F. Puss proved them wrong. When he slept in the cradle he always distanced himself from the face of the sleeping baby.

Hemingway also had a home full of cats in Florida and when he shot himself in 1961 he left behind a whole colony of these cats.

Fortunately for them this house (at 907, Whitehead Street, Key West, Florida 33040) was turned into a museum and the offspring of his original cats are now sold off as 'celebrity kittens'. Some of his cats had strange feet and today their price tag depends on how many toes they have – the seven-toed ones being the most expensive.

VICTOR HUGO

The favourite cat of the great French novelist and dramatist, Victor Hugo (1802–1885), was a 'magnificent Angora' called Gavroche. The cat was his companion when he was living on the island of Guernsey with his wife and his mistress, while waiting for the fall of Napoleon III, so that he could safely return to France. This cat was later renamed Chanoine – the canon – because it was so indolent (there being a French expression 'to lead an easy life, like a canon').

Victor Hugo marvelled at the companionship of a cat, commenting: 'God has made the cat to give man the pleasure of caressing the tiger.'

Victor Hugo's much loved cat Gavroche, renowned for his indolence. The writing below is the text quoted above.

PAUL KLEE

Swiss artist, Paul Klee (1879–1940) was so fond of cats that Marina Alberghini was able to write a whole book – *The Cosmic Cats of Paul Klee* – devoted to the subject. In it we meet a number of Klee's own pet cats, some of them photographed by himself: Mys, in 1902, a dark, long-haired cat; Nuggi, in 1905, a long-haired kitten; Fritzi, in 1921, a mackerel tabby; and Bimbo, in 1931, a white, long-haired cat.

In his pictures, we see the way he celebrated them in line and in paint. There are cats hunting by moonlight, cats dreaming of birds and, looming over the tiny humans below, a giant cat presiding over its sacred mountain. It is clear that Klee, the subtle, sensitive artist, was also sensitive to the subtleties and nuances of feline existence.

Bibliography
1993. Alberghini, M. *Il Gatto Cosmico di Paul Klee*. Felinamente, Milan.

BEVERLEY NICHOLS

The English author, composer and playwright, Beverley Nichols (1898–1983), who wrote over fifty books on a wide variety of topics, was passionate about cats and wrote several volumes specifically about them. Although he admitted to being a 'cat lover' he disliked the title because it implied he did not like other animals. Throughout his cat books he therefore used the expressions 'F' and 'Non-F' 'indicating a person who is basically feline or non-feline by nature'.

His own pet cats were, rather oddly, given numbers instead of names. In this he was influenced by the success of the perfume Chanel No. 5, as a result of which, he felt, 'numbers have acquired a subtle elegance of their own'. He called his first Siamese kitten 'Number One', and went on from there until he came to Six. There he had a problem because, when calling out 'Six', it sounded like 'Sicks', so he skipped that number and went straight to Seven. He also had trouble with 'Eight' because it had already been named Oscar before it arrived at his home. But at the time of writing about his cats he was still doggedly (if that is an appropriate word) looking forward to the arrival of 'Nine, Ten, Eleven and Twelve, who are sleeping somewhere in the womb of Time.'

Beverley Nichols is quoted as saying: 'I have a catholic taste in cats, in the sense that almost anything feline on four legs goes straight to my heart.'

Bibliography
(No date). Nichols, B. *Beverley Nichols' Cat Book*. Nelson, London.
1960. Nichols, B. *Beverley Nichols' Cats' A.B.C.* Jonathan Cape, London.
1961. Nichols, B. *Beverley Nichols' Cats' X.Y.Z.* Jonathan Cape, London.
1962. Nichols, B. *Cats in Camera*. Andre Deutsch, London.
1974. Nichols, B. *All about Cats*. Orbis, London.

FLORENCE NIGHTINGALE

The 'Lady of the Lamp', the founder of modern nursing, Florence Nightingale (1820–1910), owned sixty cats during her lifetime. They were all large Persians and she refused to travel anywhere without her current favourites. She named them after the famous men of her day, such as Disraeli, Gladstone and Bismarck.

She is quoted as saying: 'I learned the lesson of life from a little kitten of mine.' She goes on to describe how one of her little kittens stays put when approached aggressively by her biggest cat: '...the little one stands her ground; and when the old enemy comes near enough kisses his nose and makes the peace. That is the lesson of life; to kiss one's enemy's nose always standing one's ground.'

PETRARCH

The cat much loved by Petrarch (1304–1374), the Italian poet, was described as 'her master's joy in the sunshine, his solace in the shade'. According to Agnes Repplier, writing in 1901: 'When she died, her little body was carefully embalmed; and travellers who visited Arquà, the poet's home, hidden among the Euganean Hills, have stared and mocked and wondered at this poor semblance of cathood, this furless withered mummy, which, more than 500 years ago, frolicked softly in the joyousness of youth. Upon the marble slab on which she lay were cut two epigrams ... one of which gracefully commemorated the rival passions that shared Petrarch's heart.' (Translated from the Latin, it read: 'I was the greatest passion, second only to Laura.')

There are two other, alternative versions of this story. According to Timothy Bay, after Laura had died from the plague, one year after the poet had met her: 'Petrarch took the dead cat of his beloved Laura, embalmed it in the Egyptian manner, and placed it over his doorway, where it was to remain in protective vigil until his death.'

Louise Caldi, an art historian writing in 1976, paints a different picture: 'Petrarch's chief companion was his cat. When the poet died, the cat was put to death and embalmed. Today, the mummified body of the cat lies in a niche decorated with a marble cat and bearing a Latin inscription, said to have been written by the poet himself.'

Of the three versions, the first is the most convincing.

AGNES REPPLIER

The American essayist, Agnes Repplier (1855–1945), author of a total of twenty-six books on a wide variety of subjects, was one of the first writers to publish a serious historical study of the domestic cat: *The Fireside Sphinx* (1901). It was her ninth book, and the one she enjoyed the most: 'I adore it – quite impersonally – and don't dare pick it up, lest I waste my time re-reading it. That comes of doing – once in a lifetime – something one wants to do.' The book is dedicated to her cat Agrippina who, after presenting her with many offspring, died in kitten-birth. Miss Repplier, a lifelong spinster, commented: 'I preached virginity to Agrippina until I was blue in the face. But she'd howl, so I'd kiss her and put her out in the alley!' There, she was able to meet her lover, an old black tomcat of uncertain ownership.

Agnes Repplier had a strong dislike of neutered toms and recalled the days when, as a convent schoolgirl, she had misheard 'altered cats' as 'altar cats' and assumed they must have some mysterious, sacred role. In amused tones she openly envied Agrippina's beauty and sex appeal, observing that she herself was unlucky in love because she had 'nothing but brains'.

She also owned cats by the names of Banquo, Banshee, Nero and Carl, but it was Agrippina who was special and whose friendly ghost continued to sit on her desk as she wrote her many books.

Bibliography
1901. Repplier, A. *The Fireside Sphinx*. Gay and Bird, London.

1949. Stokes, G.S. *Agnes Repplier. Lady of Letters.* University of Pennsylvania Press, Philadelphia. (Reprinted by Greenwood Press, Westport, Connecticut in 1970.)

CARDINAL RICHELIEU

Known as 'the King of the King', because of his powerful influence over his monarch Louis XIII, the French statesman Cardinal Richelieu (1585–1642), was devoted to his many pet cats. They lived in a special room of their own next to his bedroom and were often allowed to sleep on his bed. He was, however, guilty of a strange double standard. Despite his passionate love for his own cats, he was an enthusiastic persecutor of witches and their feline familiars.

When he was dying he still owned fourteen cats and made generous provision for them in his will, arranging pensions both for

Two witches and their cats, as seen by a wood engraver of the early seventeenth century. The striped tail shows that the cat on the broomstick is definitely a tabby.

them and for their two attendants. We not only know the names of these cats, but also something about them as individuals:

There was Mounard le Fougueux, quarrelsome, capricious and worldly; Soumise, his favourite, a soft, gentle cat that often slept on his lap; Gazette, an indiscreet little cat; Ludovic le Cruel, a savage rat-killer; Mimi-Paillon, an angora; Felimare, who was striped like a tiger; Lucifer, black as jet; Ludoviska, a Polish cat; Rubis sur l'Ongle, who drank her milk to the last drop; Serpolet, who loved to sun himself in the window; Pyrame and Thisbe, so named because they slept entwined in one another's paws; and finally Racan and Perruque (wig), who were named after a bizarre incident at court. (This incident involved an absent-minded academic called Racan. His own cat had given birth in his discarded wig, which made an excellent nest for her newborn kittens. Racan put the wig on without noticing them and set off to see Richelieu. After talking for a while, he complained about palpitations in his head, scratched his wig and the kittens fell out at Richelieu's feet. The great statesman was so amused that he insisted on keeping them and christened them Racan and 'Wig'.)

When the Cardinal died, his wishes concerning the future of these much-loved cats were brutally ignored. As soon as he was in his grave, the soldiers of his Swiss Guard slaughtered the animals, burning them to death just as he had caused so many witches' cats to be put to the torch during his lifetime .

SHEIK MOHAMMED AL-FASSI

A nobleman from Saudi Arabia, the Sheik kept over a hundred stray cats in his multimillion dollar Florida mansion. He employed a staff of nine, including a private vet, to look after them in a suite of seven large rooms of their own. He had been horrified to discover that cats were frequently put to sleep when they were unwanted and vowed to stop this to the best of his ability, even to the extent of having doomed cats flown to his mansion from faraway American cities.

Had he known the true extent of the problem he might have given up before he began, but happily for a hundred cats he did not.

JEAN-CLAUDE SUARÈS

The Egyptian-born New York graphic designer Jean-Claude Suarès has allowed his passion for cats to develop into wide-ranging studies of cats in art, literature and photography, providing us with a fascinating group of illustrated books. Surprisingly, he reports that, when he was growing up in Egypt, the original homeland of the domestic cat: 'I was never allowed to have cats and I was never allowed to drive, so when I finally came to the United States and moved into an apartment I got a cat and a Rolls-Royce And then I started multiplying everything... so my record number of cats is thirteen and my record number of Rolls-Royces is nineteen.'

Interviewed in 1978, he mentioned that one of his cats was called Maurice because it was the name of his (then) wife's lover, who was 'not allowed on the bed either'.

Bibliography

1976. Suarès, J-C. and Chwast, S. *The Illustrated Cat*. Harmony Books, New York.

1977. Suarès, J-C. and Chwast, S. (Editors) *The Literary Cat*. Berkley Windhover Books, New York.

1981. Suarès, J-C. *Great Cats. The Who's Who of Famous Felines*. Bantam Books, New York.

1983. Suarès, J-C. *The Indispensable Cat*. Stewart, Tabori and Chang, New York. (British edition by Webb & Bower, Exeter in 1984).

1992. Suarès, J-C. (Editor) *Black and White Cats*. Collins, San Francisco.

1993. Suarès, J-C. (Editor) *Hollywood Cats*. Collins, San Francisco.

Also: *The Photographed Cat*; *The Preppy Cat*; and *The Cat Scrapbook*.

MARK TWAIN

The American humorist and author, Samuel Langhorne Clemens (1835–1910), better known by his pen name of Mark Twain, was devoted to his cats and could not imagine life without them: 'A house without a cat, a well-fed, well-petted, and properly revered cat, may be a perfect house, perhaps, but how can it prove its title.' He gave them exotic names, such as Apollinaris, Zoroaster, Blatherskite and Sour Mash, and explained why: 'names given them, not in an unfriendly spirit, but merely to practise the children in large and difficult styles of pronunciation. It was a very happy idea – I mean, for the children.'

ANDY WARHOL

The American pop artist Andy Warhol (1928–1987) was notorious for his outrageous lifestyle, but privately enjoyed quieter, more traditional moments than his public image would suggest. Among his private passions was his love of cats. This was not made public until the year after his death, when two cat books were published by his estate. Originially created in the 1950s, these books were privately printed in limited editions (of only 190 numbered copies) exclusively as gifts for his friends. They were illustrated by Warhol with uncharacteristically sentimental sketches of his cats Hester and Sam.

Bibliography
Early 1950s. Warhol, A. *Holy Cats by Andy Warhol's Mother.* Chatto and Windus, London.
c.1954. Warhol, A. *25 Cats Name Sam and One Blue Pussy.* Chatto and Windus, London.

HENRIETTE VAN WEELDE

Henriette van Weelde is not famous for herself, but for what she has done to help cats. She is the creator of one of the best known and most unusual cat sanctuaries in the world, which can still be seen today in the heart of modern Amsterdam. Her Poezenboot (Pussycat-boat) is a barge permanently moored alongside one of the city's famous canals. It was bought by her in 1969 to provide a home for the orphaned, stray, sick and rejected cats of Amsterdam, and quickly became a tourist attraction.

Originally Henriette offered her own house as a sanctuary for the strays, but soon there were far too many of them. The barge provided the answer and, at the same time, enabled visitors to see the animals and, touched by their plight, to provide much needed funds to support her work. By 1971 she was forced to expand again and bought a second barge.

The original boat now holds about 60 elderly and sickly cats who will live out the remainder of their lives on board. The second boat houses the younger and healthier cats – ones that can be re-housed and which are awaiting adoption. Since no stray cats are ever turned away, (and it has been estimated that altogether there are about 50,000 stray cats in Amsterdam), it is not surprising that a third barge is already being sought. Henriette, who is no longer young, is helped by five volunteers, but receives no financial aid from the city authorities. Her feline Noah's Ark is open to the public every day between 1 and 3pm. The address is: De Poezenboot, Singel 38 G, 1015 AB Amsterdam, Netherlands. See also www.poezenboot.nl

CARDINAL THOMAS WOLSEY

It is frequently stated that Cardinal Wolsey (1471–1530), the chief minister of Henry VIII, was a cat lover who was so attached to his pets that he insisted on taking them with him on formal occasions. According to one report, he took them to state dinners and even to church services. According to another, he always had his favourite black cat beside him on his throne when he was administering justice as Lord Chancellor of England.

Carl Van Vechten in his classic work *The Tiger in the House* (1920) comments: '…holy men as well as devils found the cat the most attractive of animals. The profound wisdom, the concealed claws, the stealthy approach, and the final spring, all seem to typify the superior attorney. We should not be astonished, therefore, that Cardinal Wolsey placed his cat by his side while acting in his judicial capacity as Lord Chancellor.'

Unfortunately, no written or pictorial evidence or reference is ever given to support these claims and it looks as though the ever-present Wolsey 'cat' may have been an invention, perhaps concocted by his enemies to suggest that he had a sinister 'Familiar'.

6

FAMOUS PET CATS

ANDY
Owned by Florida Senator Ken Myer in the 1970s, he fell from the sixteenth floor of an apartment building in Florida and survived, making him the record-holder for the longest non-lethal fall in feline history.

ARIEL
An 'orange Persian' cat owned by author Carl Van Vechten and discussed in his classic work *The Tiger in the House* (1920), where he describes its unusual love of water. Ariel would 'leap voluntarily into my warm morning tub and she particularly liked to sit in the wash-hand-bowl under the open faucet.'

He also claimed that this particular cat would retrieve a catnip mouse 'as often as I would throw it' and that she 'used to hide spools, keys, pens, pencils and scissors under the rug'.

ATOSSA
A Persian cat immortalized by the English poet Matthew Arnold (1822–1888). In his 1882 poem about his canary 'Matthias', he recalls the way his old cat Atossa would sit for hours, immobile, beside the bird's cage, never attempting to attack it, but never giving up hope:

'Cruel, but composed and bland, Dumb, inscrutable and grand,
So Tiberius might have sat, had Tiberius been a cat.'

BA-TOU

Ba-tou was an African wild cat adopted by the French novelist Colette. She wrote about the animal in her 1922 story *La Maison de Claudine*, where she commented that, although domestic cats are by nature secretive, 'Ba-tou hid nothing'. Eventually, after she found the cat caressing a puppy in a suggestively predatory manner, she accepted the inevitable and had Ba-tou dispatched to the zoo.

BEERBOHM

Beerbohm was London's longest serving theatre cat. For twenty years he was the resident mouser at the Globe theatre (now re-named the Gielgud) in London's West End and became a favourite with many of the stars who appeared there. Occasionally he would wander on stage during a play, to the delight of the audience and the dismay of the performers, who were always upstaged by his entrance.

A well-built tabby cat, he was named after Herbert Beerbohm Tree, the famous actor-manager at Her Majesty's Theatre. It was there that he was born and reared before being transferred to mousing duties at the Globe in the mid-1970s. He survived a near-fatal road accident to become famous enough to have his picture hung in the theatre's lobby. He had a close relationship with Fleur, an elegant theatrical mouser who worked at the nearby Lyric Theatre. Their vocalizations often filled the night air in Soho. He died in March 1995, after retiring to Kent with the theatre's carpenter.

BOUHAKI

Certain authors have given this particular feline the distinction of being 'the first cat known to have had a name'. It appears on an ancient Egyptian limestone wall carving dating from the XI Dynasty (1950BC). The animal is shown beneath the chair of a seated husband and wife. It is a rather strange-looking creature with a short, curled tail, a fat body with swollen teats and a rather pointed face.

According to the famous Egyptologist, Flinders Petrie, who first examined the carving, the tomb where it was placed belonged to a King An.ãa and the animal depicted is not a cat, but a pet dog. He states: '…on the tablet is the image of the king, standing, having between his feet his dog named Behukaa.'

Early cat authors have a different interpretation. Champfleury, writing in 1869, says: 'One of the most ancient representations of the cat is to be found in the necropolis of Thebes, which contains the tomb of Hana. On the stela is the statue of the King, standing erect, with his cat, Bouhaki, between his feet.' This version was repeated time and again in later cat books, until more scholarly authors turned again to the original source and rejected the feline interpretation, insisting, with Petrie, that the animal must have been a dog.

The confusion was partly caused by the fact that the stone block on which the carving was made has a picture on both sides. On one side is a standing man with his pet dog, while on the other side is the depiction of the man and his wife, seated, with the 'cat figure' beneath their chair. Clearly the two scenes have been confused over the years, but this is only part of the problem.

Egyptologists themselves are still arguing over the identity of the cat-like animal itself, and some believe that this too is a dog. To a zoologist, however, there seems little doubt that it is, in fact, meant to be a female cat in the late stages of pregnancy. There are no dog portrayals in the art of ancient Egypt that look remotely like this animal. Also, all the later examples of 'pet animal under woman's chair' are undeniably feline.

The only difficulty with this interpretation is the figure's short, curled tail, but even this is less of an obstacle than might be imagined, as this particular mutation is now known to have been rather widespread in the history of domestic cats. Alternatively, the end of its tail could have been amputated accidentally or removed for some superstitious reason. If this view is accepted, there remains the question of the cat's name. Unfortunately, the title of

A seventeenth-century drawing of an Egyptian cat.

Bouhaki belongs to the pet dog on the opposite side of the tablet.

The cat figure has no name. So, although this may well be the earliest representation of a pet house-cat anywhere in the world, it cannot sustain its popular reputation of being 'the first cat known to have had a name'. That accolade must go to a pet cat called Nedjem (meaning Sweet or Pleasant) that dates from the reign of Thutmose III (1479–1425BC).

BROWNIE

Brownie became one of the richest cats in the world in 1963 when, along with its companion, Hellcat, it inherited $415,000 (£228,250)on the death of its owner, a Dr William Grier of San Diego.

CALVIN

Calvin was a Maltese Cat who arrived one day at the home of Harriet Beecher Stowe, the American author who wrote *Uncle Tom's Cabin*. He was an assertive, gastronomic cat who, having taken over the house, never left, and frequently sat on the author's shoulder as she worked on her manuscripts. He was a dignified animal with a serene air, who 'radiated calm during the hours of frenzied writing', who was intelligent enough to learn to open doorhandles, and who was never late for meals in the dining room.

A literary friend of Stowe's, who looked after the cat when she was away, wrote of him: 'he is a reasonable cat and understands pretty much everything except binomial theorem'.

CATARINA

Catarina was a tortoiseshell cat belonging to the American author Edgar Allen Poe. She was the inspiration for his famous horror story *The Black Cat*.

When Poe's wife, Virginia, was dying of tuberculosis in the winter of 1846, the couple were destitute. A visitor found the stricken woman lying on straw 'wrapped in her husband's greatcoat with a large tortoiseshell cat in her bosom. The wonderful cat seemed conscious of her great usefulness. The coat and the cat were the sufferer's only means of warmth…'

DUSTY

Reputed to be the most prolific female cat in the world, by 1952 Dusty of Bonham in Texas had produced a total of 420 kittens.

EPONINE

Eponine was a green-eyed, black cat belonging to French poet and novelist Théophile Gautier. Her habits are recorded in his work *La Ménagerie Intime*. A 'sensitive, nervous and electric animal', she was so intelligent and sociable that she had a place set for her at the author's table.

If we are to believe Gautier, Eponine's behaviour during meals was exemplary. She was always promptly in her seat (no doubt with a little help from his servants) at the moment when he entered his dining room. She sat there, he reported, with: 'her paws folded on the tablecloth, her smooth forehead held up to be kissed, and like a well-bred little girl who is politely affectionate to relatives and older people.' The author and his cat then proceeded to dine together, the animal first lapping up soup (with some reluctance, he admits) and then feasting on fish. 'She went right through the dinner, dish by dish, from soup to dessert, waiting for her turn to be helped, and behaving with such propriety and nice manners as one would like to see in many children.'

Eponine, the adored black cat of the French poet Théophile Gautier

Bibliography
1899. Gautier, T. A *Domestic Menagerie*. Eliot Stock, London. (An English translation by Mrs William Chance of *La Ménagerie Intime*.)

FEATHERS

When Carl Van Vechten began writing his feline classic *The Tiger in the House* (1920), he acquired a new Persian kitten called Feathers. She was described by him as: 'a tortoise-shell and white smoke tabby queen, with seven toes on each front paw.' By the time he had completed the manuscript, fourteen months later, Feathers was fully grown and was already pregnant. He writes: 'When I began this book she was a kitten, a chrysanthemum-like ball of tawny, orange, white and black fuzzy fur, and now she is about to become a mother'.

She was, in effect, the 'Tiger' in the title of his famous work, and the dedication at the front of the book reads: 'For Edna Kenton... and Feathers'.

FOSS

The much-loved companion of Victorian artist and humorist Edward Lear, Foss was a less than beautiful feline with a startled expression, a bloated body and a greatly abbreviated tail. He became famous through the delightful cartoons of him drawn by Lear, who even went to the lengths of showing him in a range of heraldic postures, such as 'couchant', 'passant', 'rampant', and 'regardant'. Lear published that series of drawings under the title *The Heraldic Blazon of Foss the Cat.*

A striped tomcat, Foss arrived in the Lear household as a kitten in 1873. His tail was cut off by a servant called Giorgio because he believed that, if a cat left its tail in a house, it would never again stray from there.

'Foss rampant'

Lear was so concerned over his cat's comfort that when, late in life, he was moving to a new house in San Remo, he instructed his architects to design his new abode as an exact replica of his old one. This, he felt, would assist the cat to make the transition to the new house with the minimum of disturbance to its feline routine.

'Foss Pprpr' – purring?

When Foss died in 1887, he was honoured with a full burial in a grave in Lear's Italian garden, topped by a large tombstone informing the world (incorrectly) that he had lived to the ripe old age of 31. Why Lear chose to exaggerate his cat's lifespan in this way is not at all clear. He even confirmed the error in a letter in which he said: 'whoever has known me for 30 years has known that for all that time my cat Foss has been part of my solitary life…'

In reality, the cat was only 14 when he died. Perhaps Lear, who himself died two months later at the age of 76, was becoming confused in his final days.

HIMMY

Himmy holds the world record for the heaviest domestic cat. He was a neutered tabby cat belonging to Thomas Vyse of Redlynch, Cairns, Queensland, Australia. According to *The Guinness Book of Records* he weighed in at 46lb 15.25oz (21.3kg). Himmy died of respiratory failure, aged ten, in 1986.

In 1991 an American magazine held a contest to see if there was an American cat who could outweigh Himmy, but they failed. The mightiest feline they could locate was a tabby in Iowa called Spike, and he only managed a modest 37lb (16.8kg).

They repeated the contest in 1992, but could only come up with a Kansas tomcat called Morris, who, at 35lb (15.9kg), could not even match Spike. For the time being, Himmy's dubious record appears to be safe.

HINSE

Hinse was a tyrannical tomcat belonging to Scottish novelist Sir Walter Scott. He constantly terrorized the author's huge dogs and at dinner time clouted any hound that got in his way. Eventually, in 1826, he met his match. Tormenting a bloodhound called Nimrod once too often, he roused the animal into a violent retaliation and was killed in the ensuing fight. Scott wrote: '...cats are a mysterious kind of folk. There is more passing in their minds than we are aware of.'

HODGE

Hodge was a much loved and pampered cat owned by the great eighteenth-century lexicographer, Dr Samuel Johnson. Johnson's biographer, James Boswell, a confirmed cat hater, was clearly surprised at the trouble Johnson took over his cat, and he records that the great man himself would go out on errands to buy oysters for Hodge, rather than send his staff, 'lest the servants having that trouble should take a dislike to the poor creature.' It seems likely that Johnson was sensitive not only to his staff having to run such errands, but also to the thought that, by doing so, they might start making unfortunate comparisons between their diet and the cat's.

Like many cat owners, Dr Johnson imagined that his pet

understood his thoughts. On one occasion, he was remarking that he had had better cats than Hodge but, sensing Hodge's disapproval, quickly added, 'but he is a very fine cat, a very fine cat indeed.'

JEOFFRY

Jeoffry belonged to the tragic eighteenth-century poet Christopher Smart. A distinguished Cambridge scholar and fellow of Pembroke College, he ran into debt, sank into poverty and then became seriously ill. This affected his mind and he ended up in the living hell of solitary confinement in a London madhouse. As he languished in his dark, rat-infested cell for several years the cat Jeoffry was his only companion. He wrote a long, meandering poem which included some haunting lines about his pet: 'For I will consider my cat Jeoffry... For he is of the tribe of tiger...For he will not do destruction, if he is well-fed, neither will he spit without provocation... For he is an instrument for the children to learn benevolence upon... For every house is incompleat without him... For he is the cleanest in the use of his fore-paws of any quadrupede... For he is the quickest to the mark of any creature. For he is tenacious of his point. For he is a mixture of gravery and waggery... For there is nothing sweeter than his peace when at rest. For there is nothing brisker than his life when in motion... For he is hated by the hypocrite and miser... For he is good to think on, if a man would express himself neatly...'.

Smart eventually died in a debtors' prison in 1771.

KALLIBUNKER

Kallibunker was the founding father of the Cornish Rex breed. A red tabby with a curly coat, he was born on July 21st 1950 in an old farmhouse on Bodmin Moor in Cornwall. His owner, Mrs Nina Ennismore, mated Kallibunker back to his mother and so began the inbreeding programme that was to secure the Cornish Rex Cat for the future. Sadly, in 1956, when her collection of Rex Cats had risen to about forty, she had to reduce the numbers for economic reasons. Kallibunker, although still young, was among those she had put to sleep, but enough of his offspring survived to continue his line.

KAROUN

The 'King of Cats' ('deaf to orders, to appeals, to reproaches') to whom his owner, French author Jean Cocteau (1889–1963) dedicated his work *Drôle de Ménage*. He also used a long-haired grey cat of his acquaintance as the model for the feline costume worn by The Beast in his classic film *Beauty and the Beast*.

KIKI-LA-DOUCETTE

One of the many cats belonging to the French author Colette. Her passion for cats created a feline cult among the French intelligentsia at the turn of the century. Kiki was a grey male Angora who also appeared as a fictional, talking cat in *Sept Dialogues de Bêtes* (1903) (translated as *Barks and Purrs* in 1913). In the book Kiki debates life with a French bulldog called Toby-Chien: 'The cat is a guest and not a plaything... Try to imitate my serenity.'

KIRLEE

Kirlee was the founding father of the Devon Rex breed. The curly-coated Kirlee was born in 1960 in a field near a disused tin mine in Devon and was rescued by Miss Beryl Cox. He was used in breeding experiments with Cornish Rex cats, but the matings failed to produce curly-coated offspring. It was then realized that Kirlee possessed a new Rex gene and an inbreeding programme was started that led to the establishment of the Devon Rex as a distinct breed. Kirlee sired many litters before he was eventually killed in a road accident in 1970.

LANGBOURNE

Jeremy Bentham (1748–1832), the English philosopher who preached that human actions should be aimed at 'producing the greatest happiness for the greatest number' – a concept that has since become the norm for democratic societies – had a much-loved cat named Langbourne.

Despite his public concern for 'the greatest number' of people, in private life he seemed not to care for the company of even a small number of them. He was described as 'suffering few persons to visit him, rarely dining out', and was said to consider social activities a waste of his time. Instead he preferred the company of his adored cat and honoured the animal in a curious way by bestowing titles on him. From simple Langbourne, he became Sir John Langbourne, and was finally awarded a doctorate in divinity by his besotted owner, being given the title of The Reverend Sir John Langbourne, DD.

MA

Ma is the name of the female tabby cat who holds the official record for the oldest known domestic cat. According to *The Guinness Book of Records* she was 34 years old when she had to be put to sleep in 1957. She was owned by Alice Moore of Drewsteignton, in Devon. A tabby cat called Puss, said to have lived for 36 years, has also laid claim to the world record lifespan, but its case is less well documented.

MADAME THÉOPHILE

One of the many cats belonging to the French author Théophile Gautier (1811–1872). A 'red cat, with white breast, pink nose, and blue eyes', she was given her unusual name because she always shared the author's bed. She had a strange reaction to human music. Gautier observed that she would always listen attentively to singers that he accompanied on the piano. She was not happy, however, when high notes were struck. They probably reminded her too closely of sounds of feline distress and she did her best to silence them. Whenever a female singer reached a high A, the cat would reach out and close the songstress's mouth with her paw. There must have been something especially feline about that particular note because Gautier carried out experiments to see if he could fool the cat, but she always responded with her critical paw precisely when the note reached A.

Once, on encountering a pet parrot, she began to stalk it and was just moving in for the kill when the parrot spoke to her in a clear human voice, asking her if she had had her breakfast. This so unnerved the cat that she sneaked under the bed and refused to come out again that day.

MADAME VANITY

She belonged to the brilliant French essayist Michel de Montaigne (1533–1592), who wrote the following words about her in 1580: 'When I am playing with my Cat, who knows whether she has more sport dallying with me than I have gaming with her. We entertain one another with mutual apish tricks. If I have my hour to begin or to refuse, so has she hers.'

He was making a plea, far ahead of its time, for a less arrogant attitude when comparing ourselves with other animals. He writes with great modesty: 'Shall we say we have seen the use of a reasonable soul in no other creature but in man?' and he complains of man: 'that he ascribes divine conditions to himself, that he selects and separates himself from out the rank of other creatures... How does he know, by virtue of his understanding, the inward and secret emotions of beasts? By what comparison from them to us does he conclude the brutishness he ascribes to them?... The defect which hinders the communication between them and us, why may it not as well be in us, as in them? ...may they as well esteem us beasts, as we them?' It is tempting to think that it was his relationship with his cat that inspired Montaigne to such humility.

MARGATE

Margate was a stray black kitten who appeared on the doorstep of No. 10, Downing Street on 10th October 1953 and was immediately adopted by Prime Minister Winston Churchill, who saw it as a sign of good luck. He had just successfully delivered an important speech at Margate and named the kitten after the town. Ten days later, Margate progressed to a place of honour on his new master's bed.

MASTER'S CAT

When Charles Dickens' cat Williamina (see later entry) produced a litter and insisted on moving it into his study, the great man decided not to keep the kittens, but relented over one little female who was allowed to stay on and became known as the Master's Cat. She is said to have tried to gain his attention by snuffing out his reading candle with a deft paw.

MICETTO

Micetto had the rare distinction of being raised by a Pope. A big, black-striped, greyish-red cat, he was born in the Vatican, became the adored pet of Pope Leo XII (1760–1829) and was frequently seen nestling in the folds of the Pope's white robes. Also known as 'The Pope's Cat', he was the Pontiff's most intimate companion in the final years of his life. Micetto outlived his master and was adopted by Chateaubriand, the French ambassador to the Vatican, who took him back to France where he lived to a serene old age, 'bearing his weight of honours with graceful propriety, and hardening into arrogance only when forced to repel the undue familiarity of visitors'.

MIKE

Mike the Museum Cat (1908–1929) assisted in keeping the main gate of the British Museum in London for twenty years, from February 1909 to January 1929. His arrival at the Museum was unusual. An old Museum cat by the name of Black Jack, notorious for sharpening his claws on valuable book bindings, one day deposited at the feet of the Keeper of Egyptian cat mummies, a small object that he had been carrying in his jaws. It turned out to be a tiny kitten which was taken in by the Museum staff.

Christened Mike, he flourished and grew and eventually made friends with the gatekeeper, who allowed him to make a second home in his lodge. Mike became an adept pigeon stalker and frequently took a flapping bird to present to his human companions. They always rescued the bird, rewarded Mike, fed and watered the pigeon and then let it go. Mike continued to live this life of a working cat for year after year, and no one liked to disillusion him. Even during the austere years of the First World War, the Keeper of Mummified Cats (perhaps because of some unspoken superstition) made sure that he was properly fed. Wallis Budge, the famous archaeologist observed that: 'He preferred sole to whiting, and whiting to haddock, and sardines to herring; for cod he had no use whatever.'

A long obituary poem written by one of the British Museum officials ended with the words:

'Old Mike! Farewell! We all regret you
Although you would not let us pet you,
Of cats, the wisest, oldest, best cat
This is your motto – Requiescat.'

MINNA MINNA MOWBRAY

British publisher Michael Joseph was passionate about cats and wrote many books about them. According to him, Minna was a small, graceful, exquisitely proportioned, short-haired tortoiseshell tabby, with tiny white paws to match her piquant white face. In his book *Cat's Company*, he devotes a whole chapter to her, beginning with the words: 'Among all my cats, past and present, Minna Minna Mowbray was an outstanding personality.'

Bibliography

1930. *A Book of Cats*. Covici-Friede, New York.
1938. *Kittens and Cats*. Whitman, Wisconsin.
1943. *Charles: The Story of a Friendship*. Michael Joseph, London.
1946. *Cat's Company*. Michael Joseph, London.
1952. *Best Cat Stories*. Faber and Faber, London.

MISTY MALARKY YING YANG

This was the fancy name given to a male Siamese cat belonging to American President Jimmy Carter's daughter Amy. He lived as 'First Cat' in the White House for four years, from 1976 to 1980.

MOUMOUTTE BLANCHE

Moumoutte Blanche and her companion Moumoutte Chinoise were the subject of a book called *Lives of Two Cats* by the French novelist Pierre Loti (1850–1923). The book, which first appeared in English in 1900 and ran into many later editions, told the story of the author's life with his two cats. Blanche, a black and white Angora, had been with him for some years when he returned home from China with a stowaway kitten he called Chinoise. When the two cats were introduced, they attacked one another so savagely that Loti had to pour water over them, after which they never fought again.

MOUSCHI

Mouschi belonged to Anne Frank, the German Jewish girl who, with the posthumous publication of her *Diary of a Young Girl* in 1947, became a symbol of Jewish suffering during World War II. Having fled with her family to Amsterdam to escape Nazi persecution, she was forced to go into hiding in 1941. For three years, she and her family shared their secret hiding place with Mouschi, and two other cats known as Tommy and Boche, before being betrayed by informers.

MYOBU NO OMOTO

The Emperor Ichijo (986–1011), an early Japanese ruler, was so enamoured of his cat that when Myobu No Omoto (which means Omoto, lady-in-waiting) was chased by a dog he had the unfortunate canine exiled and its human companion imprisoned. The Emperor had begun his love affair with cats at an early age. When he was only thirteen, he had taken possession of a litter of kittens and had become so

The Cat's Dream *by Utamaro (1753–1806)*

attached to them that he insisted on his 'Left and Right Minister' rearing them and tending them in specially prepared boxes, at the Imperial Palace in Kyoto. They were given clothes and fed delicacies and rice. A court lady, known as Uma No Myobu, was appointed as their wet-nurse.

MYSOUFF I

Mysouff belonged to French novelist Alexandre Dumas (1802–1870). In his *Histoire de mes Bêtes* (1867) he describes how the cat greeted his return each evening as if it were a dog: 'The moment I set foot in the Rue de l'Ouest, he used to dance about my legs just like a dog; then careering along in front, and turning back to rejoin me, he would start back for the house.'

Dumas declared himself the 'defence lawyer' for all the homeless cats that he befriended. He founded a group called the Feline Defence League, along with Baudelaire, Maupassant and Anatole France.

MYSOUFF II

When Alexandre Dumas's cat, Mysouff II, the black and white successor to Mysouff I, was discovered in the cellar by his cook, it became an immediate favourite.

But then, one day, it unfortunately ate Dumas's entire collection of exotic birds. Instead of banishing the hungry feline, he gave it a fair trial before his guests the following Sunday. One guest pleaded the animal's defence on the grounds that the aviary door had been opened by Dumas's pet monkeys, and this was considered to be 'extenuating circumstances'. The sentence agreed upon was that the cat should serve five years' imprisonment with the monkeys in their cage. Luckily for Mysouff II, however, Dumas was shortly to find himself financially embarrassed. As a result, he had to sell the monkeys, and the cat regained its freedom.

NEMO

A Seal Point Siamese Cat belonging to British Prime Minister Harold Wilson and his wife Mary, living with the Wilson family at No. 10 Downing Street. Nemo always accompanied them on their annual holiday to the Scilly Isles – which was as far 'abroad' as they could go without running into quarantine problems. The name Nemo was taken from a boat in the Scilly Isles.

PANGUR BÁN

When an anonymous ninth-century Irish scholar wrote a poem about his pet cat, Pangur Bán, with whom he shared his study, he was unaware that it was the first ever mention of a pet cat in European literature.

The poem appears in Gaelic in the form of a marginal note in a dry academic commentary on Vergil, and reveals a close bond between the learned monk and his feline companion:

'I and Pangur Bán my cat
Tis a like task we are at;
Hunting mice is his delight
Hunting words I sit all night.
Tis a merry thing to see,
At our tasks how glad are we,
When at home we sit and find
Entertainment to our mind.
Gainst the wall he sets his eye,
Full and fierce and sharp and sly;
Gainst the wall of knowledge I
All my little wisdom try.
So in peace our tasks we ply,
Pangur Bán my cat and I;
In our arts we find our bliss,
I have mine and he has his.'

PENNY

Penny was a female African Leopard cub reared by Joy Adamson and then returned to the wild in the Shaba Reserve in Kenya. Adamson had already reared and returned a lion (Elsa) and a cheetah (Pippa), and Penny completed her trio of Africa's great cats. Penny was the most difficult and unreliable of the three. Although she took Adamson to see her cubs after she had mated with a wild leopard she was unpredictable and several times bit or clawed her foster-mother.

Bibliography
1980. Adamson, J. *Queen of Shaba*. Collins Harvill, London.

PIPPA

In Joy Adamson's book *The Spotted Sphinx* she describes the way in which she reared a pet cheetah called Pippa and then returned her to the wild. Released in the Meru National Park in Kenya, Pippa mated successfully and produced four sets of cubs before she died as a result of a fight.

Bibliography

1969. Adamson, J. *The Spotted Sphinx*. Collins Harvill, London.
1970. Adamson, J. *Pippa the Cheetah and her Cubs*. Collins Harvill, London.

POPPA

According to *The Guinness Book of Records*, Poppa was the second heaviest cat ever. An eleven-year-old male tabby from Newport in Wales, belonging to a Gladys Cooper, he tipped the scales at 44.5lb (20.19kg). The only cat to out-weigh him was an Australian tabby called Himmy (see earlier entry) who reached nearly 47lb (21.3kg).

PRESIDENTIAL CATS

A number of felines have graced the White House in Washington, as pets of various American Presidents or their families, including the following:

16th:	Abraham Lincoln (1809–1865), Tabby.	
19th:	Rutherford Hayes (1822–1893), Siam.	
26th:	Theodore Roosevelt (1858–1919), Slippers/ Tom Quartz.	
29th:	Calvin Coolidge (1872–1933), Smoky/ Tiger.	
35th:	John Kennedy (1917–1963), Tom Kitten.	
38th:	Gerald Ford (1913–), Shan.	
39th:	Jimmy Carter (1924–), Misty Malarky Ying Yang.	
40th:	Ronald Reagan (1911–2004), several un-named cats.	
42nd:	Bill Clinton (1946–), Socks.	

PUDLENKA

Karel Capek (1890–1938), the Czech playwright, felt himself to be magically infested with cats. On the very day his Angora tomcat died of poison, an avenging female cat appeared on his doorstep. Its mission, he mused, was to 'revenge and replace a hundredfold the life of that tomcat'. Christened Pudlenka, she set about this task with a reproductive verve that staggered him, producing in a very short space of time no fewer than twenty-six kittens. One of her daughters, Pudlenka II, continued with the 'plot', presenting Capek with twenty-one more kittens before she was killed by a dog. One of her daughters, named Pudlenka III, in turn continued what he called 'The Great Task' of creating a host of cats to seize power 'to rule over the universe'.

Bibliography
1940. Capek, K. *I Had a Cat and a Dog.* Allen & Unwin, London.

PULCINELLA

Pulcinella was the name of the cat belonging to the Italian composer Domenico Scarlatti (1685–1757). Pulcinella's special claim to fame rests with his habit of leaping up onto the keyboard of the composer's harpsichord and walking up and down on the keys. On one occasion this inspired Scarlatti to compose a fugue (*Fugue in G Minor*: L499), which became generally known as 'The Cat's Fugue'. Scarlatti recorded his comments on this co-operative effort:

'My cat… would walk on the keys, going up and down from one end to the other. Sometimes he would pause longer on one note listening closely until the vibration ceased. One evening, while dozing in my armchair, I was roused by the sound of the harpsichord. My cat had started his musical stroll, and he really was picking out a melodic phrase. I had a sheet of paper to hand, and transcribed his composition.'

PUSS

According to *The Guinness Book of Records*, the claim for the longest-lived of all domestic cats was on behalf of a tabby cat called Puss who died in 1939 at the amazing age of 36 years and a day. The case was not fully documented, however, and the official record has now been transferred to a female tabby called Ma, who is known to have survived for a fully authenticated 34 years.

RUMPEL

Robert Southey (1774–1843), the English author and poet who was an early figure in the Romantic movement, had such regard for his cat that he insisted on giving it a formal name that makes even the most elaborate pedigreed name seem economical. The cat's full title was: The Most Noble the Archduke Rumpelstizchen, marquis

Macbum, Earle Tomemange, Baron Raticide, Waowler, and Skaratchi. Known as Rumpel to his friends, his death caused the whole household, servants included, to mourn his passing, Southey remarking that the sense of bereavement was greater than any of them liked to admit.

SELIMA

Selima was a tortoiseshell tabby cat owned by the English man of letters, Horace Walpole (1717–1797).

With his friend, the poet Thomas Gray, he made the Grand Tour of Europe and when his beloved cat was drowned in a goldfish bowl, Gray wrote a poem to commemorate the event, called *Ode on the Death of a Favourite Cat Drowned in a Tub of Gold Fishes* (1748).

SHAN

Shan was one of those rare felines to inhabit the White House as American 'First Cat'. Most presidents, being men who enjoy power, prefer the more slavish devotion of a dog. Cats usually enter the White House as pets of the president's children and Shan was no exception, being the Siamese cat pet of President Gerald Ford's daughter Susan.

SIAM

Siam, a gift from the American Consul in Bangkok to the wife of the American President, Rutherford B. Hayes, in 1878, was the first Siamese Cat ever to reach the United States.

SIZI

Sizi belonged to the Nobel Prize-winning French missionary Albert Schweitzer (1875–1965) and lived with him at his famous clinic in Africa. Visitors noted his deep affection for the cat and the way that he pandered to its needs.

SLIPPERS

Slippers was the much-loved pet of American President Theodore Roosevelt (1858–1919). Anatomically, he was an unusual cat in having six-toed feet. A grey tabby with a self-confident, almost arrogant air, he deferred to no one as he strolled around his White House domain. His main claim to fame was that, one evening in 1906, he forced an entire procession of important White House guests to make a detour around his recumbent form, as they moved from the State Dining Room to the East Room. He frequently wandered off for days on his own, but always returned to the Presidential residence after a while, to lord it again over the mere humans who lived there.

SMOKY

Smoky was an unusual gift for American President Calvin Coolidge (1872–1933). He was not a domestic cat, but a wild bobcat caught for the President in Tennessee. Smoky was graciously accepted, but then quickly moved on to a zoo for safe-keeping. Other strange gifts he received included a female raccoon called Rebecca (which he did keep at the White House), a wallaby, a hippopotamus, a bear and a pair of lion cubs (which he did not).

SOCKS

The 'First Cat', officially belonging to Bill and Hilary Clinton, but in reality owned by their daughter Chelsea. A black and white cat, he was called Socks because of his four white feet.

When she was fourteen, Chelsea was reputed to have written a 'rap' song, which included the words: 'Socks sucks, I hate that cat. Socks sucks, worse than GATT.' It later emerged that this was the work of anarchic leftist journalist, Tom Gargola, who published the words of the song as a satirical joke against the White House.

At the peeak of his fame, Socks was reputed to receive 75,000 letters and parcels at the White House each week and 1993 saw the publication of his diary, called *Socks Goes to Washington*.

SUGAR

Sugar achieved the seemingly impossible feat of travelling 1,500 miles to be reunited with his owners. When Mr and Mrs Woods, who owned Sugar, decided to move to Oklahoma in 1951, they left the cat behind with neighbours because he hated travelling in cars. After two weeks in the neighbours' house, the cat vanished and they never saw him again. Fourteen months later he jumped though a window and onto the shoulder of Mrs Woods in her Oklahoma farm. She could hardly believe it was the same cat, but close inspection revealed that it was.

Many claims for long treks made by pet cats are simply cases of a similar cat adopting a family when it moves into a new home. The family, missing their old cat, imagines that the stray that is now purring at their feet is their original pet. In this case, there was a way to be certain, because Sugar was unmistakable. He was a cream-coloured part-Persian with a deformed left hip. When Mrs Woods examined the new arrival at her farm, she found that it was not only a cream-coloured part-Persian, but that it, too, had a deformed hip. It could not be any other cat, it had to be Sugar. How the animal had managed to navigate its way over such a vast distance to a new home (rather than back to an old, well-known one) is not clear.

TABBY

During Abraham Lincoln's presidency, his son Tad's cat Tabby became America's 'First Cat'. It is also reported that he himself adopted three orphaned cats that he found half-frozen in a tent when he was visiting General Grant's camp during the Civil War.

TAFFY

A thieving cat commemorated in Christopher Morley's 1929 poem 'In Honour of Taffy Topaz'.

TARAWOOD ANTIGONE

A female brown Burmese cat owned by Mrs Valerie Gane of Church Westcote, Kingham, Oxfordshire, which currently holds the record for producing the largest litter of kittens in recorded history: nineteen, consisting of one female, fourteen males and four stillborn. They were born on August 7th, 1970. The mother was four years old when the huge litter was delivered by Caesarean section. The father was a half-Siamese.

TIGER

One of the heaviest domestic cats in the world, according to *The Guinness Book of Records*, Tiger was a long-haired cat, part Persian, who belonged to a Mrs Phyllis Dacey of Billericay, Essex, England. His great weight – 43lb (19kg) – was recorded when he was eight years old. This is four times the average weight of an adult domestic cat. Tiger died of kidney failure in 1980.

His record was finally broken by Poppa, a male tabby who weighed 44lb (20kg) and another male tabby called Himmy who achieved an astonishing 46lb (21kg) plus.

TIGER

Tiger was the much-loved pet of the English novelist Charlotte Brontë. Homesick during a trip to Brussels in 1843, she wrote to her sister Emily that she longed to be home, in the kitchen with 'you standing by, watching that I save the best pieces of the leg of mutton for Tiger…' who '…would be jumping about the dish and carving knife…'

TIGER

Tiger was the name given to a stray cat which appeared in the grounds of the White House in Washington in the 1920s, and stayed on to become the First Cat of America. A grey-striped alley cat, he was adopted by President Calvin Coolidge who used to walk around with the animal draped about his neck. The President became so attached to him that, when Tiger once went missing, he instructed that a radio appeal should be broadcast to recover him. He was eventually tracked down in the Navy Building.

TIMOTHY

Timothy was a white cat belonging to author Dorothy L Sayers. He appears in two of her poems, 'For Timothy' and 'War Cat'.

TINKER TOY

A male Blue Point Himalayan, he holds the official record for the smallest known domestic cat, measuring only 2.75in (7cm) tall and

7.5in (19cm) long. He was owned by Katrina and Scott Forbes of Taylorville, Illinois.

TOM KITTEN

Tom Kitten was the name of the White House First Cat during the Kennedy years. He was the pet of President Kennedy's daughter Caroline, and was sufficiently famous when he died in 1962 to receive obituary notices in the press.

TOM QUARTZ

This Tom Quartz was a kitten belonging to President Theodore Roosevelt, who named him after Mark Twain's fictional cat. It lived in the White House in the early twentieth century, where it repeatedly tormented the little black terrier belonging to the President's youngest son, Quentin.

TOWSER

Towser (1963–1987) holds the record for the champion mouser of all time. A female tortoiseshell owned by Glenturret Distillery near Crieff, Tayside, she is reported to have killed an average of three mice a day, every day of her adult life, giving an estimated lifetime total of 28,899 rodents.

TRIXIE

Trixie was a black and white cat belonging to the third Earl of Southampton, in the reign of Elizabeth I. When the Earl was imprisoned in the Tower of London by the Queen, tradition has it that his devoted cat made its way across London and climbed down the chimney that led to his cell. Once there, it remained to keep him company until he was released, two years later. The Earl was so impressed with his cat's loyalty that he commissioned a portrait showing himself and his pet together in his cell.

Although cats do have a remarkable homing instinct, it is not clear how Trixie would have known where to find her owner, and the heart-warming story may have been slightly embellished during the course of time. In her biography of the Earl, Charlotte Stopes puts forward a less impressive, but more convincing suggestion that Southampton's wife was involved and: 'that it was her happy thought to take his favourite cat with her to help to comfort him'. Despite this, it is clear that however the cat did come to be in the Earl's cell, it certainly remained there to keep him company during the long dreary months of his imprisonment, because the portrait appears to have been painted towards the end of his period of incarceration, in 1603.

WHITE HEATHER

White Heather was a long-haired black and white cat that lived in luxury in Buckingham Palace. Owned by Queen Victoria in her old age, the cat outlived the Queen but managed to maintain its royal status by staying on as the pet of her son, Edward VII.

WILLIAM

A white cat, William, belonged to author Charles Dickens (1812–1870). When he produced a litter of kittens he was renamed Williamina. The litter was born in the kitchen, but the mother cat insisted on carrying them, one by one, into the great man's study. Not wishing to be disturbed, he removed them, but she persisted, bringing them back and placing them at his feet. He was forced to give in and the family was reared nearby as he worked at his desk. When the kittens had grown, he kept one of them, which was called 'The Master's Cat'.

WINDY

Wing-Commander Guy Gibson VC, the famous dam-buster of World War II, was often accompanied on his dangerous wartime missions by his pet cat Windy, 'an all-swimming and all-flying cat' who 'put in more flying hours than most cats'.

*A political cartoon lampooning Tsar Peter the Great who
made fashionable a 'Cat's Whisker' moustache
in preference to a full beard*

7

CARTOON CATS

BOOTH'S CATS

George Booth, cartoonist for *The New Yorker* and other American magazines, specializes in cat cartoons, inspired by his own feline pets, Amberson and Tata (who started out as Ambrosia and James Taylor, until it emerged that they were male and female respectively). His cat cartoons have appeared in book form with titles such as *Think Good Thoughts About a Pussy-Cat*.

COURAGEOUS CAT

A feline skit on Batman, with Courageous Cat and his assistant Minute Mouse emerging from the Cat Cave in the Cat Mobile to administer justice to a variety of villains such as The Frog and Harry the Gorilla. The animated cartoon created by Bob Kane in 1961 was seen in a series of 130 TV programmes.

DUCHESS

In Walt Disney's 1970 cartoon feature *The Aristocats*, Duchess is the elegant, sophisticated Parisian cat who is abducted and taken to the French countryside.

ESMERALDA

A black-striped, strip-cartoon cat who first appeared on December 3rd, 1933, in a Sunday comic strip by Al Smith called *Cicero's Cat*. A clever, cunning cat, Esmeralda appeared regularly for thirty years, outwitting other animals in her slapstick adventures.

FELIX

Felix the Cat was the first of the three famous animated cartoon cats. He appeared as early as 1919 in *Feline Follies* for Paramount. He went unchallenged for many years until MGM introduced *Tom and Jerry* in 1939 and Warner Brothers launched their rival, *Sylvester*, in 1945. Created by Pat Sullivan and animated by Otto Messmer, he dominated the film cartoons of the 1920s. His character was that of a resilient survivor in a hostile world. His name was derived from 'felicity' and he was deliberately designed to be a black cat who was also a hero, in order to counteract the hostile superstitions that still linked such cats to witchcraft and evil. Marcel Brion wrote of him: 'He is honest, generous, fearless, and optimistic. He is ingenious and fertile in resourcefulness... [He has] two mental attitudes: astonishment and curiosity. The virtues of poets and scholars.'

Felix appeared in several hundred animated films and had the distinction of starring in the first ever 'talkie' cartoon, even before the birth of Mickey Mouse, who was clearly a derivative figure. He also became the first moving image to be seen on television, having been used in an experimental test by NBC in 1928. In addition, he was immensely popular in strip-cartoon form in newspapers and comic books, a separate career that he began in 1923. In the 1960s he made a comeback on television, in a modernized form, with a further 260 episodes of *Felix the Cat*.

Bibliography
1991. Canemaker. J. *Felix. The Twisted Tale of the World's Most Famous Cat*. New York.

FIGARO

Figaro appears as a lively kitten belonging to the wood-carver Gepetto, in Walt Disney's 1940 feature-length cartoon film, *Pinocchio*.

FRITZ

Fritz first appeared in 1965 in strip cartoon form in underground comic books. He was created by the artist Robert Crumb, who based him on his family cat, Fred. Originally, as a teenager, he had made drawings of Fritz for private amusement, but later, in the liberated atmosphere of the 1960s, they began to appear publicly. They were sexually outrageous and caused considerable controversy. Fritz was as a different from a Disney cat as it possible to be. He mouthed endless four-letter words and added to his obscenities by undertaking blatant sexual adventures. An expert on comic-book history described the cat as 'a con-man, a sex maniac, and totally incorrigible'. Fritz developed a huge cult following, especially in the hippie subculture of the sixties. Despite the anger he caused, Crumb was solemnly described as 'a kind of American Hogarth ... who gave back to cartooning the scatological exuberance it had during the Regency...'

In 1971 a young film animator called Ralph Bakshi turned Fritz into an adult film star. His cinema feature called *Fritz the Cat* was the first ever X-rated cartoon film, full of sexually explicit material. One critic described it as 'a fast-moving orgy of outrage'. Another described it as: 'a bitter and snarling satire that refuses to curl up in anyone's lap.' When Crumb saw what Bakshi had done, he was so furious that he tried to have the film banned. When this failed, he took revenge (and neatly prevented any sequel) by drawing a cartoon strip in 1972 called Fritz the Cat 'Superstar' in which Fritz is murdered by a deranged ostrich who drives an ice pick through the lecherous cat's skull.

GARFIELD

Garfield is a strip cartoon cat whose great appeal depends entirely on the fact that he is unashamedly a complete slob. Created by Jim Davis in 1977, he is a fat, greedy, lazy, selfish and sometimes aggressive animal, but he is quite unrepentant. 'Grovelling,' he says, 'is not one of my strong suits.' He gets his own way, bites the postman, attacks dogs, hates jogging, refuses to diet, hangs from the ceiling, sleeps too much, watches too much television, hates cat food, loves lasagne, knocks things over and never apologizes. With charm like that it was inevitable that he would soon become a bestseller (*Garfield at Large*, 1980) and would be syndicated in 700 newspapers.

He later featured in the films *Garfield: The Movie* (2004) and *Garfield: A Tale of Two Kitties* (2006).

HEATHCLIFF

Heathcliff is a strip-cartoon cat, created in 1973 by artist George Gately, who commented: 'Before him, cats were depicted as either stupid or sinister. But cats are smart. Heathcliff represents the anti-hero, like Humphrey Bogart. He's a tough little mug.'

Named after the character in Emile Brontë's *Wuthering Heights*, Heathcliff steadily grew in popularity until, by 1981, he was syndicated in more than 700 newspapers. He also appeared in Saturday morning animated cartoons on ABC TV and was the subject of two books: *Heathcliff Banquet* (1980) and *Heathcliff Feast* (1981).

KRAZY CAT

Krazy Cat was a slightly surrealist strip cartoon feline invented by George Herriman in 1910. The strip broke many conventions and was never a major commercial success for the artist, but did gain him critical acclaim and considerable respect from literary quarters. President Woodrow Wilson was a devoted follower and in 1922 John Carpenter made the cat the subject of a full-length ballet. The poet e.e. cummings wrote: 'Krazy Kat is a living ideal. She is a spiritual force, inhabiting a merely real world, and the realer a merely real world happens to be, the more this living ideal becomes herself...' The strip continued for over thirty years, until Herriman's death in 1944.

Bibliography

1986. McDonnell, P. *Krazy Kat. The Comic Art of George Herriman*. New York.
1990. Herriman, G. *The Komplete Kolor Krazy Kat. Vol. 1*. 1935–36. London.
1991. Herriman, G. *The Komplete Kolor Krazy Kat. Vol. 2*. 1936–37. USA.

LUCIFER

Walt Kimball, one of Walt Disney's animators, owned a large calico (tortoiseshell and white) cat that was used as the model for Lucifer, the house cat, in Disney's feature-length cartoon, *Cinderella* (1950).

OLLIE

An orange cat with large feet, created by Harry Hargreaves in 1951 for his strip cartoon *Ollie the Alley Cat*.

O'MALLEY

O'Malley is the wily alley cat who falls in love with the beautiful Duchess in Walt Disney's 1970 feature-length cartoon film *The Aristocats*.

PUSSYCAT PRINCESS

In a comic strip created by Grace Drayton in 1935, Pussycat Princess was a kitten that ruled a domain called Tabbyland. The strip was soon taken over by Ruth Carroll, who continued with it until it finally ceased in 1947.

SPOOKY

Spooky, a black and white cat with a conspicuously bandaged tail, appeared in strip cartoons by artist Bill Holman, in the 1950s.

SYLVESTER

MGM's immense success with their *Tom and Jerry* animated cartoons for the cinema, which began in 1939, prompted Warner Brothers to create their own, rival feline. Sylvester first appeared on March 24th 1945 in *Life with Feathers*. A skinny black and white cat with a red nose and a large white ruff of fur protruding from either side of his face, he was the creation of I 'Friz' Freleng.

Just as Tom had a potential victim in the shape of the little mouse Jerry, so Sylvester had Tweety Pie, a tiny, baby-faced canary in a cage, on which to set his sights. As with Tom, the prey was never devoured, the hungry feline inevitably suffering considerably in his attempts to consummate his predatory urges.

Sylvester's voice was provided by actor Mel Blanc. The cat's inimitable catchphrase was 'Sufferin' Succotash!' The canary, who suffered from a speech impediment, was best known for 'I taut I taw a puddy tat'.

Sylvester first met the canary in a 1947 cartoon called *Tweety Pie*, for which Freleng won an Academy Award. He won another Oscar in 1957 for *Birds Anonymous* in which Sylvester attended therapy sessions in an unsuccessful attempt to give up his continual bird-addiction.

TIGER TIM

One of the very first of the cartoon cats, Tiger Tim was a playful tiger cub created by Julius Stafford Baker in 1904, making his debut in *Mrs Hippo's Kindergarten*. This was the first ever strip cartoon in a British newspaper.

TOM

In countless *Tom and Jerry* film cartoons, Tom (the cat) and Jerry (the mouse) have conducted a non-stop personal war for over half a century. The cat's repeated attempts to kill and eat the mouse are always foiled, usually with melodramatically violent retaliations by the triumphant mouse. The battling duo first appeared in an MGM animated cartoon called *Puss Gets the Boot* in 1939. They were the immensely successful creation of Fred Quimby, William Hanna and Joseph Barbera, who received no fewer than seven Oscars during the eighteen years that followed. Tom and Jerry also appeared on the pages of comic books from 1942 to 1972.

TOP CAT

An animated cartoon cat created by Hanna-Barbera for ABC TV in 1961. Top Cat (TC to his friends) is a fast-talking alley cat based on the Sergeant Bilko character. He lives in a garbage can in Manhattan with five other cats. A streetwise wheeler-dealer, he is constantly trying to improve their standard of living by various tricks and strategies.

WILEY CATT

A comic strip cat created by Walt Kelly in 1948, Wiley Catt was a Commie-hating, reactionary, shotgun-toting bobcat who lived in the Okefenokee Swamp. He appeared in Kelly's strip *Pogo* from 1948 to 1975.

8

FILM CATS

A NUMBER OF feature films have employed cats in their titles, or used them as their central theme. In most cases there is a genuine feline element in the films, and these are the ones that are listed here. Those where the use of the word 'cat' in the title is merely symbolic or metaphorical have been omitted.

It is a sad commentary on surviving feline mythology that so many cat films involve elements of mystery, killing and horror, as though the earlier witchcraft associations of cats have yet to be completely obliterated.

THE BLACK CAT
(1934, USA, B&W, Universal)
Horror film loosely based on the story by Edgar Allan Poe, starring Boris Karloff and Bela Lugosi.

THE CASE OF THE BLACK CAT
(1936, USA, B&W, Warner)
Routine Perry Mason murder mystery involving a cat.

THE BLACK CAT
(1941, USA, B&W, Universal)
Murder mystery about a cat-loving recluse, starring Basil Rathbone and Gladys Cooper.

CAT PEOPLE
(1942, USA, B&W, RKO)

Horror classic about a beautiful girl being transformed into a lethal panther. The first monster film not to show its monster, relying entirely on suggestion. Starring Simone Simon.

THE CURSE OF THE CAT PEOPLE
(1944, USA, B&W, RKO)

A sequel to the 1942 classic, with the central figure a child who is haunted by the Cat People. Starring Simone Simon.

THE CAT THAT HATED PEOPLE
(1948, USA, MGM)

A cartoon film about a Manhattan cat taking a trip to the moon.

THE BIG CAT
(1949, USA, Eagle-Lion)

Film drama set in the great outdoors, about families combining to defeat a marauding mountain lion, starring Preston Foster and Forrest Tucker.

RHUBARB
(1951, USA, Paramount)

A comedy, starring Ray Milland, about a millionaire who leaves his entire fortune, including his baseball team, to a ginger cat called Rhubarb. Rhubarb was played in the film by a professionally trained cat called Orangey, who also appeared in the 1961 film *Breakfast at Tiffany's*.

ANDROCLES AND THE LION
(1952, USA, B&W, RKO)

In ancient Rome, a slave helps a wild lion by removing a thorn from its paw. Later, in the arena, the now captive lion refuses to devour the slave. Based on the play by Shaw and starring Victor Mature and Jean Simmons.

BELL, BOOK AND CANDLE
(1958, Columbia, USA)

A romantic comedy starring James Stewart and Kim Novak, about a modern-day witch and her 'familiar,' a Siamese Cat called Pyewacket. The witch sets about seducing her neighbour by supernatural means and she does this by stroking Pyewacket while uttering magic spells.

The cat playing the role won a Patsy Award, the animal equivalent of an Oscar, for her performance. The supporting cast included James Stewart, Kim Novak and Jack Lemmon. *Bell, Book and Candle* was originally a 1950 Broadway play by John van Druton,

BREAKFAST AT TIFFANY'S
(1961, Paramount, USA)

A classic romantic comedy starring Audrey Hepburn as Holly Golightly, who lives in a New York apartment with a cat called, simply, 'Cat'. The cat is symbolic of her rootless condition. At the start of the film she says: 'Poor old cat. Poor slob. Poor slob without a name. The way I look at it, I don't have the right to give him a name.'

At the end of the film, musing on her miserable mental state, she proclaims: 'I don't know who I am. I am like Cat here. We're a couple of no-name slobs. We belong to nobody and nobody belongs to us. We don't even belong to each other.' At this point we see her abandon the cat in a rain-sodden alley, opening her taxi door on the way to the airport, and pushing him out into the downpour, shouting at him: 'This ought to be the right kind of place for a tough guy like you – garbage cans, rats galore. Scram!'

In the final, iconic scene from the film, she then relents and goes back for him, searching the alley desperately until she finds him. Our last view of her shows her clutching the sodden cat (and her boyfriend), symbolizing the change that has come over her – that she at last admits to having feelings for others.

The feline role was played by a strong-willed tom named 'Orangey,' a professional cat, trained by Frank Inn, who performed in a number of feature films, including the title role in *Rhubarb* (1951). Orangey was a tough-looking ginger cat with a fiery temperament, who often required many 'doubles' for difficult scenes. He won a Patsy, the animal equivalent of an Oscar, in 1952 and again in 1962. He died in 1963.

PUSS IN BOOTS
(1961, Mexico)
A Mexican interpretation of the well-known fairytale.

SHADOW OF THE CAT
(1961, GB, B&W, U-I)
Another 'old dark house' horror story in which the murderers of the cat's mistress are brought to justice by the animal itself.

THE INCREDIBLE JOURNEY
(1963, USA, Disney)
Three family pets, a Siamese cat and two dogs, are stranded and must make their way home over 250 miles, experiencing many adventures on the way.

ONE DAY, A CAT
(1963, Czechoslovakia)
A fantasy about a cat that wears spectacles, and the effect he has on the village where he lives when he removes them.

THE THREE LIVES OF THOMASINA
(1963, USA, Disney)
A children's film about a cat belonging to the daughter of a vet. Starring Susan Hampshire.

A TIGER WALKS
(1963, USA, Disney)
A children's film about a tiger that escapes from a circus. Starring Sabu.

UNDER THE YUM YUM TREE
(1963, USA, Columbia)
A lecherous landlord is followed around by a cat as he tries to seduce a student, in a comedy starring Jack Lemmon and Carol Lynley.

BORN FREE
(1965, GB, Columbia)
Based on the true life story of Joy Adamson and her tame lioness, Elsa, in Africa, starring Virginia McKenna and Bill Travers.

CLARENCE THE CROSS-EYED LION
(1965, USA, MGM)
An adventure comedy set in Africa and starring an amazingly well-trained, cross-eyed lion called Clarence.

Two animal trainers, Ralph Helfer and Ivan Tors, had set up a centre called 'Africa, USA' just outside Los Angeles. One day a small lion cub with a squint arrived and the idea for a gentle, lovable, leonine star was born. Clarence grew to be one of the most amenable of all tame lions and starred in the feature film *Clarence the Cross-eyed Lion* in 1965. Then, from 1966 to 1969, he went on to feature in the popular TV series *Daktari* which, although it was supposed to be set in East Africa, was filmed entirely at their compound in California.

THAT DARN CAT!
(1965,USA, Disney)
A small-town comedy with a Siamese Cat playing the central role, helping to trap bank robbers. Starring Hayley Mills.

CAT!
(1966, USA)
Children's film about a friendship between a boy and a wild cat. The boy's kindness to the cat is later rewarded when the animal saves him from danger.

EYE OF THE CAT
(1969, USA, Universal)
A cat-hating nephew attempts to murder his wealthy cat-loving aunt, but she is saved by her colony of loyal felines. Starring Eleanor Parker, Michael Sarrazin and Gayle Hunnicott.

ROBINSON CRUSOE AND THE TIGER
(1969, Mexico, Avco Embassy)

Based on the novel by Defoe, but with the addition of a pet tiger for the shipwrecked hero.

THE ARISTOCATS
(1970, USA, Disney)

Cartoon feature-length film about an attempt to rob two cats of their rightful inheritance.

FRITZ THE CAT
(1971, USA, Fritz Productions)

Adult, feature-length cartoon film notorious for its obscenity and violence, concerning the adventures of a New York alley cat called Fritz.

LIVING FREE
(1972, GB, Columbia)

Sequel to *Born Free*, continuing the dramatized biography of Joy Adamson and her tame lions in Africa, starring Susan Hampshire.

THE NIGHT OF THE THOUSAND CATS
(1972, Mexico)

A horror film about a mad aristocrat living in a castle containing a colony of man-eating cats whose favourite diet appears to be beautiful young women.

SHAMUS
(1972, Columbia, USA)

A routine murder mystery starring Burt Reynolds, Dyan Cannon and the famous TV cat 'Morris'.

HARRY AND TONTO
(1974, USA, TCF)

Harry, an elderly widower, evicted from his Manhattan apartment, sets off with Tonto, his much loved feline companion, on a long journey to California. When they finally reach there, Tonto falls sick and dies. Harry is played by Art Carney, who won an Oscar for his performance. Tonto is played by a large, eleven-year-old, ginger tabby cat with eyes the colour of marrons glacés.

I AM A CAT
(1975, Japan)
A cat's-eye view of a human family in turn-of-the-century Japan.

THE UNCANNY
(1977, Canada/GB, Rank/Cinevideo/Tor)
A collection of three horror stories about 'evil' cats, starring Peter Cushing and Ray Milland.

THE CAT FROM OUTER SPACE
(1978, USA, Disney)
A live-action Disney feature film concerning an extra-terrestrial cat of superior intelligence, called Jake, who is equipped with a magic collar. He is forced to land his spacecraft on Earth for urgent repairs. A professionally trained feline called Rumple plays the role of the alien cat. The film also features Roddy McDowall and Sandy Duncan.

ALIEN
(1979, USA, Twentieth Century Fox)
An orange tabby 'ship's cat', called Jones, lived on board the spaceship Nostromo in this science-fiction classic featuring Sigourney Weaver and John Hurt.

OUR JOHNNY
(1980, Austria)
The disruptive impact of a cat on an ordinary, peaceful family.

ROAR
(1981, USA, Noel Marshall)
Animal adventure story involving a large number of tame lions. Starring Tippi Hendren.

CAT PEOPLE
(1982, USA, Universal)

A remake of the earlier classic horror film. Whenever she makes love, a beautiful girl changes into a lethal feline and must kill in order to return to human form. Starring Nastasia Kinski and Malcolm McDowell.

THE BLACK CAT
(1985, Italy)

A paranormal mystery about a cat in an English village that may be causing the deaths of villagers.

CAT'S EYE
(1985, USA, Famous Films)

A collection of three horror stories involving cats, starring James Woods and Drew Barrymore.

DANGEROUS DESIRE
(1992, Canada, Tomcat Productions)

A male dancer with a genetic disease is treated by being injected with DNA from a domestic cat. As a result, he becomes increasingly acrobatic, sexually voracious and predatory.

SLEEPWALKERS
(1992, USA, Columbia)

A Stephen King horror story. A sleepwalker is defined as 'a nomadic shape-shifting creature of human and feline origin'. To survive they must suck the life out of virgins and to accomplish this they must first change into the shape of a big cat. A tabby cat called Clovis comes to the virgin's rescue with the help of other local cats.

THE BLACK CAT
(1993, USA, Independent)

An adaptation of Edgar Allan Poe's horror story about a man's hatred for his wife's cat.

HOMEWARD BOUND
(1993, USA, Disney)

A remake of *The Incredible Journey* of 1963, in which a cat and two dogs must find their way home after being stranded. The voice of the cat Sassy is played by Sally Fields.

THE LION KING
(1994, USA, Disney)

A feature-length cartoon film in the Walt Disney tradition, telling the story of the trials of a young lion cub called Simba, following the death of his father.

HOMEWARD BOUND II: LOST IN SAN FRANCISCO
(1996, USA, Disney)

In this sequel, the cat Sassy and her two canine companions get lost at the airport when they are supposed to be setting off for a holiday in Canada with their owners. The voice of the cat Sassy is again played by Sally Fields.

THE LION KING II: SIMBA'S PRIDE
(1994, USA, Disney)

A sequel to *The Lion King*, with Simba now an adult lion who has a daughter called Kiara. Kiara befriends a male cub from a rival pride and this leads to the inevitable emotional conflicts.

STUART LITTLE
(1999, USA, Colombia)

A children's film, employing computer animation, about a family who adopt a talking mouse. The family cat, called Snowbell, wants to kill the mouse. Nathan Lane plays the cat's voice.

CATS AND DOGS
(2001, USA, Warner Brothers)

A comedy in which we find a war is being waged in our homes that we don't even know about – a violent struggle between two great armies: the Cats and the Dogs. There is a feline plan afoot to destroy a new vaccine that, if successfully developed, would destroy all human allergies to dogs.

STUART LITTLE 2
(2002, USA, Colombia)

In this computer animated sequel, Stuart, the talking mouse adopted by the Little family, rescues a canary from a falcon, but one day, the canary is nowhere to be found, so Stuart and Snowbell, the family cat, set out across the city to find her.

THE CAT IN THE HAT
(2003, USA, Universal)

Based on the Dr Seuss classic, the film tells the story of two bored children visited by a talking cat, played by Mike Myers, who causes chaos.

THE CAT RETURNS
(2004, Japan, Studio Ghibli)

A dubbed English language version of the 2002 Japanese cartoon film *Neko no ongaeshi*. A young girl rescues a mysterious cat from traffic and soon finds herself the unwelcome recipient of gifts from the King of the Cats, who also wants her to marry his son, Prince Lune. The girl visits the cat kingdom and narrowly escapes again.

SHREK 2
(2004, USA, Dream Works)

In the original animation comedy, *Shrek*, we meet a reclusive ogre and a chatterbox donkey who go on a quest to rescue a princess for a tyrannical midget lord.

In the sequel, Shrek, the ogre, and Fiona, the princess, have married, but Fiona's father, the king, is unhappy about this and hires a cat called Puss in Boots, a sword-fighting feline and skilled ogre-slayer, to kill Shrek. The voice of the cat is played by Antonio Banderas.

TWO BROTHERS (DEUX FRÈRES)
(2004, France, Fox Pathé Europa)

A film by the brilliant Fench director, Jean-Jacques Annaud. It follows the adventures of twin tiger cubs who are born in the wild. Separated, one of them is sold off to a circus, while the other becomes the companion of the governor's young son. Later, when they are both fully grown, they find themselves pitted against one another in a brutal, staged tiger fight.

GARFIELD: THE MOVIE
(2004, USA, Twentieth Century Fox)

Based on the classic comic book character, this animated film sees the famously lazy pet cat deeply upset by the arrival of a dog in the family home. But when the dog is kidnapped, Garfield feels responsible and sets off to rescue him. The voice of the cat is played by Bill Murray.

GARFIELD: A TALE OF TWO KITTIES
(2006, USA, Twentieth Century Fox)

In this sequel, Garfield's owner travels to England and inadvertently takes his pet cat along for the trip. A case of mistaken identity finds Garfield confused with a posh, castle-owning cat. Garfield again has the voice of Bill Murray.

And finally, two historic cats that cannot be linked to a single film:

PEPPER

The very first film star cat, Pepper was a grey alley-cat who appeared in early Mack Sennett comedies with Charlie Chaplin, Fatty Arbuckle and the Keystone Cops. She appeared one day on the set of a film and was promptly written into the story. After many starring roles, she went into decline following the death of her favourite co-star, a Great Dane called Teddy. She refused all replacements for Teddy and soon vanished as mysteriously as she had arrived.

LEO

The trademark lion of MGM productions, who roars an introduction at the start of each film. The first time Leo appeared was in 1928, with MGM's first sound movie, called *White Shadows in the South Seas*. The idea of using a feline emblem in this way came from a young advertising executive called Howard Dietz.

Several male lions have been used in this role in the history of the company, starting with one called Slats, then Jackie and finally, in colour, one named Tanner. Jackie, who was born in the Los Angeles Zoo, was perhaps the most famous of these, having had a long performing career: he acted as Leo the Lion for MGM for nearly eighteen years, appearing in more than 250 films.

9

TELEVISION CATS

ARTHUR

Arthur was hired by Spillers, the British petfood company, in the 1960s because he could scoop his food out of a tin with his paw. Between 1966 and 1975 he appeared in 309 TV commercials.

Such was Arthur's fame that, according to one report, Spillers bought him outright for £700 ($1,250). Contradicting this, a young actor claimed that Arthur was still his, and a bitter custody battle began in the High Court. On the first day of the court case, Arthur was missing and the young actor insisted that the animal had sought asylum in the Russian Embassy. A Russian spokesman denied this, rather angrily pointing out that the Soviets had better things to do than worry about high-earning, capitalist felines. With Arthur still invisible, the actor was jailed for two weeks for contempt of court. The day after he went to jail, Arthur mysteriously re-surfaced and was handed back to Spillers. The case dragged on for two years, with the actor claiming damages to the tune of £150,000 ($268,500). He failed in this attempt, and at last Arthur was the secure property of the petfood company.

The cat's professional life blossomed. He moved into T-shirts and towels and other advertising campaigns. He even had his autobiography ghosted for him by author John Montgomery. After a long and successful professional career, he finally died in February 1976, just before his seventeenth birthday.

Ten years later, animal trainer Ann Head found a replacement for Arthur. She was inspecting the animals at the Wood Green Animal

Shelter in north London when she spotted a skinny, bedraggled white cat called Snowy. The vet had given him 48 hours to live, but Ann took him home and, nursing him day and night, carefully brought him back to full health.

It is surprising that he survived, as he was found to be suffering from malnutrition, various parasites including worms, an eye infection, ear mites, eczema and a cold. But she persevered and, two months later, fully recovered and re-named, he was making his first TV commercial.

His first public appearance was in January 1987 at the Savoy Hotel in London, where he was launched as Spillers' second Arthur. Like the original Arthur, Arthur II was able to scoop food out of a catfood tin with his paw, and also use it in other ways. In response to the command 'paw', he would place his left foot on anything near to him. Ann Head has always been at pains to point out that she used rewards rather than punishments in the training of Arthur II, and that he was never starved before the filming of a commercial, as some people seem to think.

Nine years after Ann Head discovered Arthur II, feeling that his long and successful career was coming to an end, she commented: 'Now the time has come for him to "put his paws up" and take it easy. There is a youngster waiting in the wings to take over the role and, by an incredible coincidence, he is yet another Snowy from the Wood Green Animal Shelter. The dynasty lives on.'

The long saga of Arthur I and Arthur II has a remarkably close parallel in the United States, in the story of Morris I and Morris II (see next page).

Bibliography
1970. *Dudley*, E. Arthur. Frederick Muller, London.
1975. Montgomery, J. *Arthur the Television Cat*. WH Allen, London.
1995. Head, A. *Arthur's World of Cats*. Lennard Publishing, Harpenden, Herts.

MINERVA
Fictional character featured in the television programme *Our Miss Brooks*.

MORRIS

Morris was a large, stray ginger tom discovered in an animal shelter in a Chicago suburb in 1968. Professional animal trainer Bob Martwick paid five dollars for him, which rescued him from 'death row'. Twenty minutes later and it would have been too late.

The 'big orange tiger' was estimated to be about seven years old and was chosen for his haughty, unflappable personality. He appeared arrogantly calm, as though he owned the place, and was not alarmed even when Martwick deliberately dropped a metal dish nearby.

At first he was appropriately named Lucky but when he was chosen to promote a brand of catfood on television in 1969 he was renamed Morris. He appeared in forty commercials during the next ten years, before his death in 1978, and became nationally famous throughout the United States. His gimmick was that he was exceptionally finicky over his food, and would only eat the very best.

His rags to riches life story appealed to the American public and Morris was treated like the great star he had become. He travelled by limousine, guested on TV talk shows, attracted a huge fan mail, ate out at exclusive restaurants in the company of attractive young (feline) queens, visited the White House, met the Hollywood elite, and even had an outrageously expensive Louis Vuitton litter box. In 1972 he starred in a Hollywood movie called *Shamus* with Burt Reynolds and Dyan Cannon. In 1973 he was awarded a Patsy, the animal equivalent of an Oscar, and in 1974 was the subject of a biography by Mary Daniels. He died in 1978 and was replaced by Morris II after a nationwide search that took two and a half years.

Morris II, who was also discovered at an animal rescue shelter, looked exactly like the original Morris, and shared his stoical, patiently aloof personality. He was so similar that it was hard to tell them apart on the screen, and the catfood commercials could continue once more. Morris II also had his biography written, this time by Barbara Burn, who was astonished at the long lines of people queuing in the rain to see the cat star at book signings during the launch of her book.

In 1988 Morris II became a candidate for the Presidency of the United States on the grounds that he was better known than almost any of the other candidates. On August 18th, he held a press conference in Washington to announce his candidacy and outline his political platform, which had a great deal to say on the subject of feline rights. Despite a spirited 'Morris for President' campaign, he was beaten by a whisker. Although high hopes that he might at last bring a more civilized, elegant air to the Oval Office were dashed, all was not lost, because his brief entry into politics indirectly gave a great boost to his reputation in the field of catfood advertising. And with $1.4 billion spent on catfood annually in the USA, such a career is not to be sneered at.

Bibliography
1974. Daniels, M. *Morris. An Intimate Biography*. William Morrow, New York.
1980. Burn, B. *The Morris Approach*. New York.

MTM KITTEN
The kitten appears in the logo of the Mary Tyler Moore television production company, as a parody of the famous MGM roaring lion.

10

FICTIONAL CATS

BROBDINGNAGIAN CAT

A gigantic domestic cat, 'three times larger than an ox', encountered by Lemuel Gulliver in Part II of Jonathan Swift's (1726) book *Gulliver's Travels*.

BUSTOPHER JONES

'The Cat About Town' from T S Eliot's 1939 *Old Possum's Book of Practical Cats*. An immaculate, night-clubbing cat whose story begins:

> 'Bustopher Jones is not skin and bones – In fact, he's remarkably fat.
> He doesn't haunt pubs – he has eight or nine clubs, For he's the St James's Street Cat…'

CATASAUQUA

A female Manx Cat invented by Mark Twain in a bedtime story for his daughters. She first appeared in print in *Letters from the Earth*.

CAT IN THE HAT

The Cat in the Hat is the alarming feline at the core of Dr Seuss's children's story of the same name. The cat decides to keep two bored children entertained while their mother is away. Chaos is caused by the cat's antics, but the magical feline manages to return everything to normal before the mother returns.

Dr Seuss is the pen-name of Theodor Seuss Geisel.

Bibliography

1957. Geisel, T.S. *The Cat in the Hat*. Random House, New York.
1958. Geisel, T.S. *The Cat in the Hat Comes Back*. Random House, New York.
1969. Geisel, T.S. *I Can Lick 30 Tigers Today*. Random House, New York.

CAT THAT WALKED BY HIMSELF

'The Cat that Walked by Himself' is the title of a tale by Rudyard Kipling (1865–1936) in his *Just So Stories* (1902) in which he creates a fable to epitomize the personality of the domestic cat – part tame companion and part independent spirit. After the dog, the horse and the cow have agreed to become domesticated, the cat holds out for the wild life. But then it finally appears at the human den and says: 'I am not a friend, and I am not a servant, I am the cat who walks by himself and I wish to come into your cave.' Some hard bargaining follows in which the cat promises to catch mice 'for always and always and always; but still I am the cat that walks by himself…'

CHESHIRE CAT

In chapter six of Lewis Carroll's *Alice's Adventures in Wonderland* (1865) a large cat is encountered, lying on a hearth and grinning from ear to ear. Alice asks: 'Please would you tell me why your cat grins like that?' The only answer she gets is: 'It's a Cheshire cat and that's why.' There is no explanation as to why cats from that particular English county should be prone to smiling. A clue comes with the final disappearance of the cat, when it slowly vanishes, starting with the end of its tail and ending with the broad grin, which remains some time after the rest of the animal has gone. It is this disembodied grin that some authorities claim explains the source of Lewis Carroll's image, for there used to be a special kind of Cheshire cheese which had a grinning feline face marked on one end of it. The rest of the cat was omitted by the cheese-maker, giving the impression that all but the grin had vanished.

Lewis Carroll may well have seen these cheeses. But he may have taken his reference from an even earlier source.

The reason why the Cheshire cheese-makers saw fit to add a grinning cat to their product was because the expression 'grin like a

Cheshire cat' was already in use for another reason altogether. It was an abbreviation of 'grin like a Cheshire Caterling', which was current about five centuries ago. Caterling was a lethal swordsman in the time of Richard III, a protector of the Royal Forests who was renowned for his evil grin, a grin that became even broader when he was dispatching a poacher with his trusty sword. Caterling soon became shortened to 'Cat' and anyone adopting a particularly wicked smile was said to be 'grinning like a Cheshire Cat'. Lewis Carroll possibly knew of this phrase but, because he refers to the grin outlasting the rest of the body, it is more likely that his real influence was the cheese rather than the swordsman.

A third, but less favoured, explanation has been offered, namely that one of the leading families in Cheshire had the face of a lion as part of its coat of arms. In the hands of local sign painters, the lion's image gradually got to look like a grinning cat.

Whichever is the true origin, the fact remains that the saying does not start with Carroll, as most people assume, but was in reality much older and was merely borrowed and made famous by him.

COWARDLY LION

In Frank Baum's fantasy *The Wonderful Wizard of Oz* (1900), the Cowardly Lion joins the expedition to find the wizard in order to gain some courage. At the end of the quest, the wizard pours it from a green bottle into a dish. The lion laps it up until he is 'full of courage' and then retires to the jungle to become king of the forest.

In the 1939 MGM film version of the story, the lion was played by Bert Lahr.

CYPRIAN CAT

'The Cyprian Cat' (1940) is the title of a short horror story by mystery writer Dorothy L Sayers.

A man who is terrified of cats stays at an inn owned by a friend of his. Outside the inn, every night, a circle of cats gathers, dominated by the Cyprian Cat. Later, this cat climbs up to the man's closed window, but cannot get in. When there is a thunderstorm, he opens his window and the Cyprian Cat enters his bedroom. He hits it and at that very moment, his friend's wife falls sick. The next night, when the cat enters his room again, he shoots it and his friend's wife falls dead.

DICK WHITTINGTON'S CAT

There are those who feel that Dick Whittington's famous cat was a factual feline, but the evidence is against this. The popular legend of the cat, which was based on a much earlier fable, runs as follows:

A poor orphan boy called Dick Whittington sets out for London where he hopes to make his fortune. He has been told that the streets of the city are paved with gold, but instead he finds only hardship and nearly starves to death. He is saved by a rich merchant called Hugh Fitzwarren who puts him to work in his kitchen. The boy's room is infested with rats and mice and to get rid of them he buys a cat for a penny from a little girl he meets in the street. The cat succeeds at its task and Dick becomes extremely fond of his feline companion. But then his employer asks him to let his cat travel on one of his trading ships, the *Unicorn*, to control the vermin on board. Dick is unhappy about losing the company of his cat, but finally, with great reluctance, he agrees.

At this point in the story, Dick is treated badly by the cook in the kitchen where he works and decides to run away. Just as he is leaving the city, on Highgate Hill (where today there is a bronze statue of his cat), he hears the pealing of Bow bells and they seem to say to him, 'Turn again, Whittington, Lord Mayor of London.' This strange experience persuades him to return to the city.

An engraving of the famous cat, published in 1777

When the ship on which his much loved cat is sailing reaches its destination on the Barbary coast, the animal is sold for a huge sum to a Moorish ruler. The Moorish court is overrun with rodents and the cat's destructive impact is so impressive that the price paid for it is ten times that offered for the whole of the rest of the cargo. With this money, young Dick's fortune is made and he is able to marry Alice, his employer's daughter. He continues to improve his position in society until he eventually becomes Lord Mayor of London.

This story has been told and retold, and has even become enshrined as the theme of a popular British pantomime. Although it is widely believed to have been based on the truth, it is in reality an invention. Significantly, the story does not appear until 1605, over 200 years after the events it describes, and is a completely garbled version of the events that led up to the installation of Dick Whittington as Lord Mayor.

Far from being a poor orphan boy, young Dick was in fact the son of a Gloucestershire knight, Sir William Whittington. In London, Dick became an important mercer, a dealer in expensive textile fabrics. He supplied velvets and damasks to the nobility, including his future king. His success relied heavily on the purchase of favours, a form of bribery which in those days was called 'achat' (pronounced 'a-cat'). (The wording of a popular ballad refers to his meteoric rise to fame and 'how his rise was by a cat'.)

So it would seem that the 'cat' had nothing to do with the feline world, but instead referred to his somewhat dubious business methods. These were so successful that he soon became immensely rich. Indeed, he was able to make large loans to both King Henry IV and Henry V. On his death he bequeathed his enormous fortune to charity. He rose to become Lord Mayor of London three times: 1397–99, 1406–07 and 1419–20. In 1416 he also became Member of Parliament for London. He married Alice, daughter of Sir Ivo Fitzwaryn, and he died in 1423. Those are the facts of his life, as far as they can be ascertained, and it would seem that the popular feline element was added at a much later date as a satirical comment. In the process, his 'cat', or bribery, became transformed into a real feline, giving us a delightful but entirely fictitious folktale.

A portrait of Whittington by Reginald Elstrock, dating from roughly 1590, showing him with his cat, was doctored to pander to public opinion. In the original version, his right hand rested upon a skull. In the modified version, the skull was replaced by a cat.

(An alternative theory proposes that Whittington's cat was an abbreviation of 'cat-boat'. A cat-boat, often spoken of simply as a 'cat', was a ketch employed to bring coal up the Thames to London. It is suggested that this enterprise was the true source of Whittington's wealth and that the boat was therefore 'the cat that made his fortune'. This is highly unlikely, as the business on which his fortune was based was concerned with fine materials rather than fuel.)

Dick Whittington and his cat from about 1700

DINAH

A mother cat with two kittens who appears as Alice's pet cat in both *Alice's Adventures in Wonderland* (1865) and *Through the Looking-Glass* (1872) by Lewis Carroll. As she is falling down the rabbit-hole at the start of her adventures in Wonderland, Alice worries aloud about Dinah, the family cat she has left behind, and debates with herself the question 'Do cats eat bats?'

At both the start and the end of the looking-glass adventure, Dinah's two kittens, a black one called Kitty and a white one called Snowdrop, play an important role in the story, and are featured in the Tenniel illustrations.

FANCHETTE

Appears in Colette's *Claudine à l'école* (1900) and *Claudine à Paris* (1901), where she is described as 'the most intelligent cat in the world'. She had a powerful sexual urge and was eventually provided with a mate because 'the poor darling wanted it so cruel'.

FLYBALL

The hero of Ruthven Todd's *Space Cat* (1952), Flyball was an intelligent, resourceful cat who saved his human companion's life during their first trip to the moon. He learned to communicate telepathically with his captain and even managed to mate with the last of the Martian cats, a horizontally striped female by the name of Moofa, producing an interplanetary litter of kittens.

GINGER

A yellow tomcat created by Beatrix Potter for her story *Ginger and Pickles* (1909). Pickles is a terrier with whom Ginger runs a small village shop for the other animals. The problem is how to avoid alarming the customers. The problem is solved by the terrier always serving the mice and the cat always attending to the rabbits.

The two owners were extremely generous, but gave so much credit that they soon went out of business.

GUS

Gus was an elderly theatre cat, well into his anecdotage, who loved to reminisce nostalgically about the good old days: 'When I made history as... the Fiend of the Fell.' He appears in T S Eliot's *Old Possum's Book of Practical Cats*. His name is said to be an abbreviation of asparagus.

HAMILCAR

Hamilcar was the acutely observed Angora cat belonging to Bonnard in Anatole France's novel *Le Crime de Sylvestre Bonnard* (1881).

HIDDIGEIGEI

The sable-coated tomcat featured in Joseph Viktor von Scheffel's famous poem 'Der Trompeter von Säckingen' (1854), which ran to over 250 editions. Hiddigeigei takes a superior view of the human race – 'contemptuous mortals' – and considers the struggle and strife of their lives quite absurd. He himself prefers the contemplative life, sitting serenely on a roof, watching the world go by. Perhaps echoing this philosophy, a restaurant in Capri was named after him.

JENNIE

A scrawny, stray tabby featured in the work of author Paul Gallico, first appearing in his story about a boy who had been turned into a cat. The story was called *The Abandoned* in the USA, and *Jennie* in the Britain (both 1950). Jennie (full name Jennie Baldrin) teaches the boy how to behave like a cat: how to fall on his feet, catch a mouse, kill a rat and defend himself.

LADY JANE

A rather sinister, large grey cat that appears in the 1853 novel *Bleak House*, by Charles Dickens.

MACAVITY

Macavity was the mystery cat in T S Eliot's *Old Possum's Book of Practical Cats*. More a cat burglar than a cat, he was a tall, thin, ginger cat who always managed to disappear at the crucial moment:

'For he's a fiend in human shape, a monster of depravity.
You may meet him in a by-street, you may see him in the square,
But when a crime's discovered, then Macavity's not there!'

MEHITABEL

New York columnist Don Marquis (1878–1937) invented a literate cockroach called 'archy' who wrote, with great difficulty on Marquis's typewriter, a series of poems and stories about a female alley cat called 'mehitabel'. The cockroach was not heavy enough to be able to create capital letters or punctuation, which gave the writings a highly characteristic style. For example, 'the song of mehitabel' is introduced by archy with these words:

'this is the song of mehitabel/of mehitabel the alley cat/as I wrote you before boss/mehitabel is a believer in the pythagorean/ theory of the transmigration/of the souls and she claims/that formerly her spirit/was incarnated in the body/of cleopatra/that was a long time ago/and one must not be/surprised if mehitabel/has forgotten some of her/more regal manners.'

The adventures of 'archy and mehitabel' appeared in countless newspaper columns over many years and were published in three volumes that appeared in many editions from the late 1920s onwards.

Bibliography

1927. Marquis, D. *archy and mehitabel*. Doubleday Page, New York.
1933. Marquis, D. *archy's life of mehitabel*. Doubleday Doran, New York.
1935. Marquis, D. *archy does his part*. Doubleday Doran, New York.

MINNALOUSHE

'Minnaloushe creeps through the grass
Alone, important and wise
And lifts to the changing moon
His changing eyes'

wrote the Irish poet W B Yeats in his 1919 poem 'The Cat and the Moon'. The reverence in which Yeats held cats is clear from the story told of him that, on one occasion, finding a cat asleep on his fur coat when he went to collect it at the Abbey Theatre in Dublin, he cut off a piece of the coat rather than disturb the animal's slumbers.

MINON

Minon is the enchanted cat in Charles Lamb's poem 'Prince Dorus' (1811).

MISTIGRIS

The cat who appears in Balzac's story *Le Père Goriot* (1835).

MONSIEUR TIBAULT

In Stephen Vincent Benét's story *The King of Cats* (1929), Monsieur Tibault is the amazing feline who, when conducting an orchestra, faces the audience and uses his tail as a baton.

MOPPET

Moppet was the title cat in Beatrix Potter's 1906 children's story *The Story of Miss Moppet*. She also appears in the 1907 story *The Tale of Tom Kitten*.

NITCHEVO

Appears in Tennessee Williams' 1948 story *The Malediction*.

PLUTO

Pluto is a tormented pet that features in the macabre tale *The Black Cat* (1843) by American author Edgar Allan Poe. At first loved and protected, the cat is later treated more and more cruelly, as its owner sinks into drunkenness and madness. When, being harshly grabbed, it responds by biting its owner's hand, he reacts by cutting out one of its eyes. Eventually he kills the unfortunate animal and is afterwards haunted by an avenging, demonic black cat who brings him to justice for the murder of his wife.

The title was used for a famous 1934 horror movie, starring Boris Karloff and Bela Lugosi, but little of Poe's original tale survived the Hollywood treatment.

POETRY CATS

There is a voluminous body of feline poetry, some incisive and illuminating and some quirky and amusing. Most, however, is unashamedly sentimental. Individual poems are to be found in the many anthologies of cat writings, but there are also a number of books devoted exclusively to feline poetry. They include the following:

1891. Brown, H. *Catoninetails. A Domestic Epic.* Lawrence and Bullen, London.

1892. Tomson, G. *Concerning Cats.* London.

1927. Marquis, D. *archy and mehitabel.* Doubleday Page, New York.

1939. Eliot, T S. *Old Possum's Book of Practical Cats.* Faber and Faber, London.

1946. Gooden, M. (Editor) *The Poet's Cat.* Harrap, London.

1947. Pitter, R. *On Cats.* Cresset Press, London.

1949. Fyfe, H. *Poems in Praise of Cats.* Bannisdale, London.

1974. Carr, S (Editor). *The Poetry of Cats.* Batsford, London. (Enlarged edition in 1980)

1984. Elson, D. *Cats! Cats!* Windmill Press, Kingswood, Surrey.

1986. Zakani, O (Translated by Basil Bunting). *The Pious Cat.* Bertram Rota, London.

1987. Joseph, M A. *Book of Cats.* Ashford Press, Southampton.

1991. Anon. *101 Favourite Cat Poems.* Contemporary Books, USA.

1992. Aldiss, B. *Home Life with Cats.* Grafton, London.

1993. Dean, J. *Tabby Tales.* Kipper Press, Lancing, West Sussex.

PRACTICAL CATS

These are the cats invented by the poet T S Eliot in the 1930s in his famous publication *Old Possum's Book of Practical Cats.* They include such well known feline personalities as Macavity, Mungojerrie and Rumpelteazer, and the Rum Tum Tugger.

PUSSY-CAT

Edward Lear's nonsense cat in *The Owl and the Pussy-cat*, who 'danced to the light of the moon', inspired by the author's own much loved cat, Foss.

RAMINAGROBIS

In La Fontaine's seventeenth-century fables, this fat, reclusive cat appears in several tales, always allowing simple, predatory greed to

overcome the finer points of philosophy. When two animals ask him to settle a dispute for them, he solves their problem by eating them both. When asked by a young mouse to wait until it is a bigger and therefore better meal, he declines the offer. When a mouse asks some rats to save him, Raminagrobis already has the small rodent halfway down his throat by the time the rats' protest group has arrived.

*A German woodcut of the
fifteenth century*

La Fontaine (1621–1695) borrowed the name of his cat from the earlier works of Francis Rabelais, where Raminagrobis was 'a Man that is both Old and a Poet', who is approached for a wise judgement.

RATON

Another of La Fontaine's cats, this one appears in the famous cautionary tale of the monkey and the cat. The monkey flatters the cat into pulling hot chestnuts out of the fire with its paw. As it is doing so, the monkey quickly eats them. The animals are then disturbed and have to flee, leaving the cat pondering the value of flattery.

RHUBARB

In the 1946 satire by American author, H Allen Smith, called *Rhubarb*, a cat of this name inherited a fortune including a New York baseball team.

In 1951 Paramount turned the novel into a feature film, with a professional acting cat called Orangey playing the title role. Orangey was a difficult and temperamental star. His co-star was the seasoned actor Ray Milland, to whom the animal took an instant dislike. Milland had to suffer the indignity of being smeared with meat paste and catnip to keep the cantankerous feline close enough to complete the filming. Orangey won a Patsy (the animal equivalent of an Oscar) for his part in the film. Despite his gallant efforts and extreme tolerance, Mr Milland won nothing.

RODILARD

In two of La Fontaine's seventeenth-century fables, the cunning, predatory cat Rodilard is doing battle with a colony of mice. In one tale, they take council and decide that the only solution is to put a bell around his neck, so that they can hear when he is approaching. The only problem is, which one of them is going 'to bell the cat'?

In the other tale, Rodilard plays dead to catch the mice and then camouflages himself with flour. Both his stratagems are successful. The name of La Fontaine's cat was borrowed from the even earlier writings of Rabelais (see below).

RODILARDUS

In the remarkable writings of Francis Rabelais (1494–1553), there appears a large, furry cat called Rodilardus (the name being a Latin rendering of 'I gnaw bacon').

In the chapter entitled 'How Panurge beray'd himself for Fear, and of the huge Cat Rodilardus, which he took for a puny devil', Rabelais describes how, when the guns of the vessel in which Panurge is sailing are fired in salute, he is below decks. Both he and the cat appear to have reacted badly to the sudden noise, because: 'Panurge like a wild addle-pated giddy Goat, sallies out of the Bread-room in his Shirt, with nothing else about him but one of his Stockings, half on half off, about his Heel, like a rough-footed Pigeon, his Hair and Beard all bepowdered with Crums of Bread, in which he had been over Head and Ears, and a huge and mighty Puss partly wrapt up in his other stocking.'

As he stands there 'scar'd, appall'd, shivering, raving, staring, beray'd, and torn with the Claws of the famous Cat Rodilardus,' he is asked about the cat. He replies: 'With this cat …the Devil scratch me, if I did not think it had been a young Soft-chin'd Devil which, with this same stocking instead of Mitten, I had snatched up in the great Hutch of Hell…'

With this 'he threw the Boar-Cat down' blaming Rodilardus for his dishevelled state, rather than his own panic.

SAHA

Saha was 'The Cat' in the title of Colette's novel *La Chatte* (1933). The story is based on the concept of 'love me, love my cat'.

Saha, a magnificent pedigree Russian Blue Cat, is so disliked by her owner's new wife, that disaster is guaranteed. The wife tries to kill the cat by pushing her off a ninth-floor balcony, but the falling animal is saved by an awning. The husband discovers what has happened and promptly goes home to mother, taking his beloved cat with him.

SAM

Yet another horror short story about cats, Walter de la Mare's 'Broomsticks' tells how a black cat called Sam, belonging to a Miss Chauncey, starts to act strangely whenever there is a crescent moon, insisting on going outside. Miss Chauncey hears cackling and other strange noises. In the morning there is the impression of a broomstick on the ground.

SHERE KHAN

In Rudyard Kipling's classic story *The Jungle Book* (1894), Shere Khan is the lame tiger who repeatedly attempts to carry off and devour the man-cub Mowgli, but without success. In the end he is killed by Mowgli who corners him in a ravine where he is trampled to death by cattle.

SIMPKIN

One of Beatrix Potter's feline characters, Simpkin appeared in *The Tailor of Gloucester* in 1903.

SUSAN

One of Beatrix Potter's feline characters, Susan is the white cat that appears in *The Tale of Little Pig Robinson* (1930).

TABITHA TWITCHIT

A fretful mother cat in several of Beatrix Potter's books for children. Her kittens were Mittens, Moppet and Tom Kitten, who were smacked and sent to their rooms when they annoyed her.

TAO

A male Siamese, who plays a central role in *The Incredible Journey* (1961) by Sheila Burnford. The cat and two dogs – Bodger, a Bull Terrier and Luath, a Labrador – become separated from their owners and must make an arduous, 250 mile journey to return home. The cat is depicted as resourceful, fearless and an excellent hunter. The book was made into a successful feature film by Walt Disney in 1963.

THOMASINA

In Paul Gallico's *Thomasina: The Cat Who Thought She Was God* (1957), the central figure is a female ginger cat who belongs to a vet's daughter. Thinking that she is ill, he decides to put her to sleep. She does not, however, die from the anaesthetic and is saved by a stranger. Coming round from the anaesthetic, the cat is convinced that she has been reincarnated as an Egyptian cat goddess.

Believing that her beloved cat is dead, the vet's daughter becomes deeply depressed and even suicidal. When she lies dying, the cat, now fully recovered, struggles home through a terrible storm to save her life.

In 1963, the story was used as the basis for a feature film by Walt Disney called *The Three Lives of Thomasina*, starring Susan Hampshire and Patrick McGoohan.

TIB

A female farmyard tabby cat, Tib features in an otherwise excessively canine story, *The Hundred and One Dalmatians* (1956) by Dodie Smith. According to the plot, young puppies are being systematically stolen for their skins and Tib is active in helping to find the missing animals. In 1961 the story was made into a cartoon feature film by Walt Disney.

TIBERT

Tibert the Cat was one of the victims of the wily fox in the twelfth-century epic *Reynard the Fox*. Sent to bring Reynard before an angry king, the fox agrees to go with Tibert, but suggests that he might like a tasty meal of mice before setting off. The cat is directed to a barn to catch the mice, only to find himself caught in a snare that had been set to trap the chicken-thieving fox.

Tibert is badly beaten by the priest who owns the barn, who leaps out of bed when he hears the yowling of the cat, and runs naked to kill the intruder. As Tibert is being attacked, he retaliates by biting off one of the priest's testicles, much to Reynard's amusement.

The cat just manages to escape death and struggles back to the court to tell the king what has happened. The fox is condemned to death and the story ends with Tibert the Cat sitting on top of the gallows and holding the rope tight as Reynard is hanged.

TIGGER

The 'Large and Helpful Tigger' from A A Milne's classic children's tale *The House at Pooh Corner* (1928), Tigger was a tiger-like feline who was described as 'a very bouncy animal'. The other animals tried to 'unbounce' him, but failed.

TOM KITTEN

Created by children's fiction author Beatrix Potter in 1907 and introduced in *The Tale of Tom Kitten*: 'Once upon a time there were three little kittens and their names were Mittens, Tom Kitten and Moppet…'

TOM QUARTZ

Tom Quartz played an important role in Mark Twain's story 'Roughing It' (1872). After his owner, Dick Baker, switched from gold mining to quartz mining, the cat was accidentally blown up when the prospectors were dynamiting some rocks. As the rocks exploded upwards, 'right dead in the center of it was old Tom Quartz a goin' end over end'. When he fell back to earth two and a half minutes later, he glared at the men and then marched off home with great dignity, but 'very prejudiced against quartz mining'.

WEBSTER

An imposing, aristocratic feline, large and black (whose 'ancestors had conducted their decorous courtship beneath the shadow of cathedrals…'), invented by P G Wodehouse, and described in delightful detail in *The Story of Webster*. The cat's bearing was so refined, and his poise so exquisite, that he made humans feel clumsy and uncomfortable in his dignified presence.

WILLIAM

William was an invention of American humorist James Thurber in his story *The Cat in the Lifeboat* (1956). A cat with a large ego, he imagined that he was the Will referred to in 'Last Will and Testament'. Taken on a round-the-world voyage, he encountered a terrible storm. As the ship was sinking he heard the cry 'William and Children first' and immediately leapt into the lifeboat, only to be thrown out by an irate sailor. When he swam ashore on a remote island he was so shocked that he could not remember his name.

ZAPAQUILDA

In Lope de Vega's epic poem *The Battle of the Cats* (*Gatomaquaia*, 1634), Zapaquilda is the feline heroine who is abducted on her wedding day and taken to the villain's castle. The poem is a feline satire on the theme of the literary epic.

*England, 1839. An engraving of an advertising card describing
amusements performed by cats*

11

WORKING CATS

SOME CATS BECOME famous, not because of their owners, but because of the place where they work, or because of the special work that they do. They include the following:

CASTLE CATS

Many British castles still house resident cats whose official duties include reducing the rodent populations. However, now that most of these great buildings have become tourist attractions, complete with restaurants, snackbars and picnic areas, their feline occupants have enjoyed an unexpected softening of their lifestyle. For example, Sumo, the huge ginger-and-white tomcat who patrols the castle grounds and 35 acres of gardens at Hever Castle, where Henry VIII so ardently courted the ill-fated Ann Boleyn, has become so well-fed that the water-fowl around the castle moat completely ignore his approach.

Bibliography
1995. Surman, R. *Castle Cats of Britain and Ireland*. Harper Collins, London. (There are two similar, previous books on working cats by the same author, called *Cathedral Cats* (1993) and *College Cats* (1994).)

CONVENT CATS

In Cyprus, the Byzantine convent of St Nicholas of the Cats today houses only five nuns but has a feline population of over 200 cats. Although the animals are traditionally tended by the nuns, most of them live semi-wild. The convent is situated near the British military base at Akrotiri, on the south coast of Cyprus, not far from Limassol. The feline community there is an ancient one, dating back to the fourth century. At the beginning of that century there had been a disastrous drought on the island, which had decimated the human population. The long years of drought had also resulted in an infestation of dangerous local snakes. When St Helena of the Cross, the mother of King Constantine the Great, visited the island in AD328, she became aware of this problem and persuaded her son to take action. He appointed Calocaerus, the chief of his camel corps, as governor of the island and Calocaerus arranged for a special group of serpent-killing cats to be brought there from Egypt. The cats were taken to the Akrotiri peninsula which is still known today as the Cape of Cats (Cape Gata). There they were cared for by the monks of the then active monastery of St Nicholas. According to legend there were soon over 1,000 of these snake-hunting felines.

The cats apparently carried out their duties efficiently, and survived well over the centuries. A Venetian monk who visited the island in 1484 reported that, between Limassol and the Cape, 'the soil produces so many snakes that men cannot till it, or work without hurt thereon… At this place there is a Greek monastery which rears an infinite number of cats, which wage unceasing war with these snakes… Nearly all are maimed by the snakes: one has lost a nose, another an ear; the skin of one is torn, another is lame; one is blind of one eye, another of both.' He records that the monks summoned the cats to eat by tolling a bell. After their meal, they then trooped back outside again to continue their ceaseless battle with the serpents.

Writing a century later, in 1580, Father Stephen Lusignan mentions that the Basilian monks who originally occupied St Nicholas of the Cats were presented with all the surrounding land: 'on one condition, namely that they should be under obligation to maintain always at least a hundred cats and to provide some food for them every day in the morning and evening at the ringing of a small bell, to the intent that they should not eat nothing but venom and that for the rest of the day and night they should go a-hunting for those serpents.'

Eventually, with the Turkish conquest of Cyprus in the sixteenth century, the monastery fell into ruins and many of the cats died of starvation. After a period of abandonment, the present Greek Orthodox convent was established to give new life to St Nicholas of the Cats, with nuns replacing the monks in the role of cat protectors, and providing a continuing sanctuary for the descendants of the feline survivors of the ancient monastery.

Despite the best efforts of the nuns, however, by 1994 the cat population was in poor condition. Many of the animals were diseased and others were emaciated and suffering from malnutrition. The colony was breeding so fast that it was impossible for the sisters to keep up an adequate food supply. Tourists visiting the convent were horrified by the condition of the cats and the WSPA (the World Society for the Protection of Animals) was called in to help. They caught up the cats, medicated them, treated their wounds, neutered 63 females and then released them all again. Regular food supplies were also arranged and at last the famous Convent Cats of Cyprus were healthy and secure for the future.

ALGONQUIN CATS

These are the famous hotel cats of New York. One of them, Hamlet, has been specially honoured as the subject of a book called *Algonquin Cat* (1980). A cat of mixed parentage, white with grey blotches and a tabby tail, he was for many years cat-in-residence, mascot and pest-controller of the famous Algonquin Hotel at 59 West 44th Street in Manhattan.

Hamlet was the replacement for Rusty, who presided at the hotel during its famous literary 'Round Table Club' days, when it was the meeting place of the great wits of New York, including Dorothy Parker, Alexander Woollcott, James Thurber and Robert Benchley.

Each Algonquin cat becomes a character in its own right and has its own special door, giving access to the hotel kitchens. One of the later recruits, in the 1990s, was an adopted stray called Matilda who, during one of her nocturnal Manhattan prowls, was mugged and had her collar stolen, an event perhaps symptomatic of her decade.

DOWNING STREET CATS

A number of working cats have made their home in the official Downing Street residence of the British prime minister over the years. One of them, a large black and white cat called Wilberforce, proved to have greater staying power than his distinguished owners. A resident mouser at No. 10, Downing Street, Wilberforce outlasted several prime ministers, carrying out his pest-control duties during the occupancies of Edward Heath, Harold Wilson, James Callaghan and Margaret Thatcher (who is rumoured to have purchased a tin of pilchards for him during her state visit to Russia). After he appeared on television with Mrs Thatcher he received more fan mail than his owner.

Wilberforce was acquired as a kitten from Hounslow RSPCA in 1973 and naming him became an immediate problem. Rival political factions insisted that he should be called Winston, Disraeli, Gladstone, Pitt or Walpole. Eventually, the caretaker of No. 10, irritated by the over-enthusiastic member of the Disraeli lobby, looked up at the bust of William Wilberforce, the man who had fought for twenty years to abolish the slave trade, and announced 'The cat is called Wilberforce'. He began a campaign of terror against the Downing Street mice that was so successful that they evacuated the premises and moved to the Home Office, where the custom of keeping a resident mouser had unwisely been abandoned.

After thirteen years of service on the staff of No. 10, Wilberforce was retired to the country where he turned his attention to dominating a large dog, interrupting this pursuit only occasionally for press calls at No. 10. Two years later, his death prompted glowing obituaries. *Cat World* reported: 'the best mouser in Britain died peacefully in his sleep on 19 May 1988'.

Wilberforce's replacement was a tom called Humphrey. A long-haired cat, also black and white, he was an adopted stray who arrived at No. 10 Downing Street in 1989 as the official mouser during the premiership of Margaret Thatcher. He outlasted Mrs Thatcher and remained at his post during John Major's occupancy. When he was accused of killing and eating four baby robins in the garden of No. 10, he was defended by his new owner, who announced on television that 'it is quite certain that Humphrey is not a serial killer.'

Then, in 1995, Humphrey disappeared. In September it was assumed that he had gone away to die in a quiet corner, probably from kidney failure due to his habit of consuming large quantities of civil service biscuits. When his probable death was published in *The Times*, the staff of the Royal Army Medical College, situated one mile from No.10, realized that the cat they had adopted and christened PC, and had fed for some months, was no ordinary stray. He was quickly returned and welcomed back (with international television coverage) to his official role as the First Mouser of the British Isles. Like his namesake (Sir Humphrey in the BBC TV series *Yes, Minister*), he was clearly a survivor.

His official role finally came to an end in November 1997, when he was apparently retired for medical reasons. There were rumours, however, that the prime minister's wife, Cherie Blair, disliked cats and had had him put down. She denied this, but an official question was asked in the House of Commons, a Conservative MP demanding proof that the 'Chief Mouser to the Cabinet Office' was still alive. As a result (and with cat-lovers' votes no doubt in mind), Downing Street went to the length of inviting press photographers to a house in South London, where the retired Humphrey was photographed with copies of the day's newspapers, to prove his continued existence. Humphrey's health must have improved in retirement, because he lived on until March 2006, when he died of kidney failure.

Bibliography
1995. Brawn, D. *A Day in the Life of Humphrey the Downing Street Cat.* Harper/Collins, London.
1986. Sturgis, M. *The English Cat at Home.* Chatto & Windus, London. (For Wilberforce)

LIBRARY CATS

Attacks by mice on valuable books have often proved a hazard for libraries. In the vast library of one of the palaces of St Petersburg the problem was so great that no fewer than 300 Russian cats were employed to control the rodent population.

In more recent times, so many public libraries in the United States have kept a resident cat, that in 1987 a group of librarians formed 'The Library Cat Society' (LCS) and issued a quarterly newsletter called *The Library Cat*. The society's creed was simple: 'We advocate the establishment of cats in libraries and recognize the need to respect and to care for library cats.'

This demand for respect for library cats might seem a trifle unnecessary, but the peaceful silence of the public library is sometimes disturbed by the arrival of a virulent ailurophobe. One such cat hater created a scandal when she demanded a tax rebate because she was unable to enter her public library in Woodford, Connecticut, because she was allergic to the library cat, a black and white female called Fred.

The library staff resisted the demand that 'Fred must go!' and the matter went as high as the state governor. Then a local schoolgirl started a 'Save Fred' petition which quickly involved everyone in the town, then in the State and finally internationally, with signatures coming from as far away as Switzerland and the Philippines.

Fred stayed, and became a star, appearing on American television, and being written about in *People* magazine and *The New York Times*. She became a major tourist attraction until her death in 1986 at the age of 14. The following year a tree was planted outside the library in Fred's memory. Appropriately, it was a Pussy Willow.

Bibliography
1992. Lahti, P. (Editor) *Cats, Librarians and Libraries*. Haworth Press, New York. Specialist Club: Library Cat Society, PO Box 274, Moorhead, MN 56560, USA.

CHAMPION MOUSERS

Mickey was a tabby cat belonging to Shepherd and Sons of Burscough, Lancashire. A champion mouser, he died in 1967 aged 23, after killing an estimated 22,000 mice.

His record was finally broken by a tortoiseshell cat called Towser, who dispatched over 28,000 at a Tayside distillery before she died in 1987 (see Chapter 6, Famous Pet Cats).

POST OFFICE CATS

It is not generally known that there are official Post Office Cats, employed to protect letters and sacks of mail from the attacks of rats and mice. These government employees have existed in Britain for over 120 years and there has been a long, official correspondence concerning them, which has been delightfully gathered together by the author Russell Ash.

Because, in earlier days, it was a common practice to send food parcels through the mail, rodents quickly became a major hazard. It was dangerous to scatter rat poison around the letters and parcels that were going to end up in people's homes – often on their kitchen tables. Traps were also a risk, especially in confined areas where so much sorting and handling of material was going on. Cats were the only solution.

In the summer of 1868, a large number of money orders were eaten by mice and the Controller of the Money Order Office promptly put in a formal request for three cats to be officially appointed to prevent this from happening again. He asked for two shillings a week to cover this, but was beaten down to one shilling by the Secretary of the Post Office, who pointed out that the animals should not be over-fed, or they would not catch their quota of mice. He added that if they failed in their duties, their allowance would be further reduced.

This type of correspondence – nearly always quibbling over the feline rates of pay – continued for year after year, with the full weight of bureaucratic precision behind it. A century later, the weekly cost of a cat had risen to ten shillings. By the mid-eighties the figure had risen to £2 ($3.60) a week.

Generally, the feline task force appears to have proved a success and it is recorded that, at one time, a total of no fewer than 25,000 cats were employed in the Post Office Service throughout the country. Their minimum wage was always a problem, however, and the staff concerned frequently had to make their voices heard. One official complained that the collecting of the cats' food was a heavy burden to bear and that 'wear and tear of shoe leather in going to and fro will cost at least one fourth of the proposed allowance' and that whatever may be left over will not 'compensate him for the loss of dignity in carrying the cats' food through the streets in Her Majesty's uniform.' Such are the hazards of working with government-appointed felines.

Bibliography
1986. Ash, R. *Dear Cats. The Post Office Letters.* Pavilion Books, London.

REFRIGERATOR CATS

Refrigerator Cat is the name that was given to a special breed of felines developed in Pittsburgh in the late nineteenth century to control the rodent pests in large commercial refrigeration plants. Arguing that some species of wild cats, such as the Canadian Lynx, live in the frozen north, it was felt that a breed of domestic cats could be developed that would be able to survive at very low temperatures. This was deemed necessary because a race of rats had managed to do just this and were causing havoc with the stored food.

The experiment was successful, American authorities reporting that 'This hardy race of Eskimo cats cannot stand the daylight nor normal temperature, but due to the cold have acquired heavily furred coats, thick tails like Persians, and tufted ears, with altogether a northern and lynxlike appearance.'

They even managed to breed in the icy conditions and the offspring were then supplied to other cold-storage warehouses.

STABLE CATS

It has often been said that in modern times cats have had only two functions – as pest controller and as pets. But there is a third, albeit much less common role that they can play. Thoroughbred racehorses are notoriously highly strung and some trainers have found that providing them with feline stable companions helps to calm them down. Daunt, the famous winner of the 1945 Derby, was said to be inseparable from a tomcat called Ginger.

George Stubbs, in his portrait of the famous stallion, the *Godolphin Arabian*, who died in 1753, includes his companion black cat in the picture (although for some reason he shows it as a tabby). When the horse died, the cat remained with its body, refusing to move. It continued to sit on the carcass until it was buried. It then crept reluctantly away and hid in the hayloft where it, too, was soon found dead.

In the 1930s, a champion horse called Fet, who won the Cesarewitch three times, insisted on having two stable companions, a goat and a black tomcat. Unless both were present at the end of the day, he became agitated and refused to bed down for the night.

Another champion horse, called Foxhall, after he had been rubbed down in his stable, used to allow two young cats to sleep curled up on his back.

The importance of companion cats to racehorses was the basis of a story by P G Wodehouse in which Wooster and Jeeves must prevent the catnapping of a stable companion. If they fail, the favourite will become so distraught that he will be unable to win the race on the following day.

THE RITZ CAT

A working feline called Tiger, also known as 'The Terror of the Ritz', was a huge tomcat employed as a mouser at the famous Ritz Hotel in London's West End. Unfortunately, he was given so many titbits and fed such a luxurious diet that he had to be sent away annually for a slimming course.

12

CATS IN ART

MANY GREAT ARTISTS have included cats in their work, and some have made them the main subject of particular paintings or sculptures. They include: Leonardo da Vinci, Boucher, Watteau, Delacroix, Géricault, Rubens, Manet, Gainsborough, Reynolds, Courbet, Renoir, Vuillard, Bonnard, Gaugin, Franz Marc, Marie Laurencin, Paul Klee, Picasso, Giacometti, Balthus, Leonor Fini, Lucien Freud, Andy Warhol and David Hockney.

Less famous artists who have become well known especially for their cat studies include: Gottfried Mind (1768–1814), an eccentric hunchback from Berne, Switzerland, over-enthusiastically called 'the Raphael of Cats'; Japanese artist Tsugouharu Foujita (1886–1968); Dutch-born Henrietta Ronner (1821–1909), the epitome of the sentimental Victorian artist; Frenchman Théophile Steinlen (1859–1923) whose Parisian cat posters became collectors' items; and British illustrator Louis Wain (1860–1939), whose anthropomorphic felines are loved by some and detested by others.

Bibliography

A number of books have been devoted to the subject of cat art. They include the following:

A drawing by 'the Raphael of Cats'

1892. Spielmann, M H. *Henrietta Ronner. Painter of Cats and Cat Life*. Cassell, London.

1970. Fish, E. *The Cat in Art*. Lerner, Minneapolis.

1974. McClinton, K M. *Antique Cats for Collectors*. Lutterworth Press, London.

1976. Suarès, J-C. and Chwast, S. *The Illustrated Cat*. Harmony Books, New York.

1976. Johnson, B. *American Cat-alogue. The Cat in American Folk Art*. Avon Books, New York.

1981. O'Neill, J P. *Metropolitan Cats*. Abrams, New York.

1981. Steinlen. *Des Chats. Images sans Parole*. Flammarion, Paris. (Libro reprint)

1984. Fournier, K. and Lehmann, J. *Chats Naïfs*. Galerie Naïfs et Primitifs, Paris.

1984. Muncaster, A and Yanow, E. *The Cat Made me Buy It!* Crown, New York.

1985. Fournier, K and Lehmann, J. *All Our Cats*. Dutton, New York.(Revised edition of *Chats Naïfs*.)

1986. Muncaster, A and Sawyer, E. *The Cat Sold It!* Crown, New York.

1987. Foucart-Walter, E and Rosenberg, P. *Le Chat et la Palette*. Adam Biro, Paris.

1988. Foucart-Walter, E and Rosenberg, P. *The Painted Cat*. Rizzoli, New York.(English version of *Le Chat et la Palette*.)

1989. Leman, M. *Martin Leman's Cats*. Pelham Books, London.

1991. Bryant, M. *The Artful Cat*. Quarto, London.

1991. Silvester, J and Mobbs, A. *A Catland Companion*. Michael O'Mara, London.

1992. Martins, P. *A Brush With Cats*. Souvenir Press, London.

1994. Busch, H. and Silver, B. *Why Cats Paint*. Ten Speed Press, Berkeley, California.(An amusing spoof book about paintings by cats.)

1994. Howard, T. *The Illustrated Cat*. Grange Books, London.

There has also been an excellent series of Cats in Art diaries, published by Alan Hutchison, London (annually from 1986 to 1992) and Four Seasons Publishing, London (1995), and a number of Cats in Art address books, also by Hutchison, London. All are heavily illustrated with colour plates of paintings featuring cats.

CATS IN ADVERTISING

Cats have figured prominently in advertising campaigns for over a century. From the brilliant posters of Toulouse-Lautrec and Théophile Steinlen in Paris in the late nineteenth century, right through to the highly professional TV performances of the famous feline petfood purveyors, Morris I & II (in the USA) and Arthur I & II (in Britain) in the late twentieth century, cats have been featured time and again by advertisers wishing to trap the attention of a preoccupied public. (See Chapter 9, Television Cats.)

Two Chicago-based Americans have collected together, in three volumes, a wide range of colourful examples of these illustrative uses of the cat. Alice Muncaster is an advertising and promotion manager for one of America's largest financial institutions. Her co-author, Ellen Yanow (later to become Ellen Yanow Sawyer) is the executive director of a national humane organization. Their collection of 'cats in advertising art' is the most extensive in the world, as their 1980s trilogy has ably demonstrated.

Bibliography

1984. Muncaster, A and Yanow, E. *The Cat Made me Buy It!* Crown, New York.

1986. Muncaster, A and Sawyer, E. *The Cat Sold It!* Crown, New York.

1988. Muncaster, A and Sawyer, E. *The Black Cat Made me Buy It!* Crown, New York.

CAROUSEL CATS

A Carousel Cat is a painted, wood-carved figure large enough to carry a human rider.

Fairground carousels or roundabouts have used a number of different animal models in the past. The original and most common was, of course, the horse, but riders were eventually offered a choice of other wooden steeds, including several felines. Lions and tigers were the most popular, but two wood carvers working in the United States did produce a number of gigantic domestic cats. These were fashioned by craftsmen at the Hershell-Spillman Company and the Dentzel Carousel Works.

According to American author Staci Layne Wilson, it was the Dentzel carver Salvatore 'Cherni' Cerniglario who created the best cats: playful animals, usually with a fish, frog, bird or squid held in their jaws. Sadly, from the 1920s onwards these original wood-carved figures were gradually phased out and today all carousel animals are made of fibreglass. (Only 300 of the 9,000 early wooden carousels are still operating.)

The antique wooden cats, some of which were saved when the old carousels were broken up, are now recognized as a major form of folk art, and have become collectors' items. One was sold at auction in 1992 for $27,500 (£15,125). (Further information is available from the American Carousel Society, Dept CF, 470 S Pleasant Ave, Ridgewood, New Jersey, 07450, USA.)

CERAMIC CATS

From the seventeenth century onwards, small ceramic figurines of cats have been popular ornaments both in the West and the Orient. The peak period, however, was the eighteenth century and the most dedicated collectors of feline artefacts focus on that epoch.

The favourite pose for these decorative cat figures is squatting with the front legs straight, and with the face of the animal turned towards the spectator. In heraldic terms this would be called *sejant guardant* – sitting and watching. Among the major types of ceramic cat are the following:

Chelsea cats: English, eighteenth century. These, the earliest of the English porcelain cats, were imitations of the expensive Meissen Cats. Most were made in the period between 1750 and 1760.

Ch'ing cats: Chinese, seventeenth to nineteenth century. Many porcelain cats were made in the K'ang-Hsi period of Ch'ing, between 1662 and 1722. They were followed later by the Chinese Export Porcelain Cats. These were eighteenth- and nineteenth-century figures from the Ch'ien-Lung period, 1736–1795, and the Chia-Ch'ing period, 1796–1821. Further examples were made in the late nineteenth century.

Delft cats: Dutch, seventeenth century and onwards. Several English centres made Delft ware pottery cats, but the finest ones were made in Holland in the eighteenth century.

Derby cats: English, late eighteenth to early nineteenth century (up to 1848). Derby and Rockingham (see below), between them, made most of the English ceramic cats.

Gallé cats: French, late nineteenth century. Gaily painted pottery cats made at Nancy in the 1890s. One of Emile Gallé's cats was recently sold at auction for £4,000 ($7,200).

Jackfield cats: English, eighteenth century. Pottery cats made in Shropshire between 1740 and 1780, with later imitations produced elsewhere.

Meissen cats: German, eighteenth century. Generally considered to be the most important of all the ceramic cats, most of their porcelain feline figurines were made between 1740 and 1765.

Rockingham cats: English, early nineteenth century. Their brown-glazed cat figures were made mostly between 1810 and 1830, although some date from as early as 1780.

Royal Copenhagen cats: Danish, nineteenth century.

Staffordshire cats: English, eighteenth and nineteenth century. Pottery cats made from about 1715 until 1750.

Wemyss cats: Scottish, late nineteenth century. Originally made at the Fife of Gallatown pottery from about 1895. Also made later, in England in the 1930s, at the Bovey Tracy pottery in Devon.

Whieldon cats: English, eighteenth century. Mottled, tortoiseshell pottery cats made between 1740 and 1780.

And that reminds me. There's a little lesson I want to teach *you*, while we're looking at this picture of Alice and the Cat. Now don't be in a bad temper about it, my dear Child! It's a very *little* lesson indeed!

Do you see that Fox-Glove growing close to the tree? And do you know why it's called a *Fox*-Glove? Perhaps you

Bibliography
1974. McClinton, K M. *Antique Cats for Collectors*. Lutterworth, London.
1996. Tenent, R. 'Cats for Collectors'. In: *Cat World Annual*, 1996. p.42–43.

HERALDIC CATS

Domestic cats are uncommon in heraldry, where the only felines to hold a prominent position are lions and leopards. The reason is not hard to find. Throughout the Middle Ages the cat was so detested by the Christian Church that it was difficult for it to be displayed as a noble image. Even at other times it was not particularly favoured in this role. There were exceptions, however, including the following:

1   In the Temple of Liberty that Rome owed to Tiberius Gracchus, the goddess was shown with a cat at her feet representing liberty.

2   The Vandals and the Suevi carried a cat sable upon their armorial bearings.

3   St Clotilda (470–545), daughter of Chilperic, King of Burgundy, and wife of Clovis, King of the Franks, had a cat sable upon her armorial bearings, in the act of springing at a rat.

4   A Catanach book plate shows a cat beneath the words 'Touch not the Cat Gloveless'.

5   The Katzen family shield shows, on azure, a cat sable holding a mouse sable in its mouth.

6   In Scotland, the Clan Chattan, whose chief was known as Mohr au Chat (great wild cat) used a cat as its emblem, with the words 'Touch not the cat but (without) the glove'.

7   In the sixteenth century, Melchior Sessa, the Venetian printer, adopted the device of a cat holding a rat in its jaws.

8   The Chetaldie family, in the Limoges country, bore, on azure, two cats argent.

9   The Neapolitan noble house of Della Gatta bore, on azure, a cat argent with a lapel gules in chief.

10   The Chaffardon family bore, on azure, three cats, or two full-face.

11   St Ives, the patron of lawyers, is shown accompanied by a cat, which is therefore seen as the symbol of the officials of justice.

12   The armorial bearings of Scotsman Peter Duguid-M'Combie of Aberdeen show a cat rearing up in the *sejant erect* position.

The amorial bearings of 'Cluny' Macpherson

13   The armorial bearings of Alfred Scott Scott-Gatty, with the motto *Cate at Caute*, show two cats in the rampant guardant position.

14   The armorial bearings of 'Cluny' Macpherson show a cat in the *sejant proper* position, beneath the words 'Touch not the Cat Bot (without) a Glove' – see left.

15   The armorial bearings of Joseph Andrew Keates show three cats in the *passant guardant* position, beneath a tiger in the same posture.

16   The coat of arms of Madame Myrtle Farquharson of Invercauld, Chief of the Clan in 1936, shows two Scottish wild cats embracing a central lozenge.

17   The Arms of the Royal Burgh of Dornoch, granted in 1929, carry the motto 'Without Feare' above a striped wild cat showing aggressively lowered ears.

The Arms of the Royal Burgh of Dornoch

CAT INN SIGNS

In the British Isles, inns, taverns and pubs have for centuries displayed their presence by pictorial sign-boards. Cats rarely featured on the earlier examples of these, probably because the buildings date from the period when felines were being widely persecuted. A number did exist, however, and some of those early ones can still be seen today. The dates given below indicate known references to particular inns:

Cat: a London tavern in Long Lane. (1636)

Cat: a London tavern in Rose Street. (1730s–1744)

Cat and Bagpipes: a London tavern on the corner of Downing Street, Westminster, where the clerks of the Foreign Office used to drink. (1810–26) Its name comes from the nursery rhyme: 'A cat came fiddling out of a barn, with a pair of bagpipes under her arm…'

Cat and Bagpipes: a pub near Moate, Kings Co, Ireland. (1866)
Cat and Fiddle: a London tavern in Shire Lane near Temple Bar. (1702–14) The name is thought to be a corruption of a thirteenth-century French phrase: *Caton Le Fidèle*, meaning 'The Faithful Knight'. The name *Caton* was given by the French to a knight who

A cat and fiddle, with a spoon running away behind

successfully defended the town of Calais for Edward I. An alternative explanation is that Cat and Fiddle is derived from *La Chatte Fidèle*, meaning The Faithful Cat, which was the name given by a Frenchman to his hotel, in honour of his cat Mignonette. A third explanation is that the old game of 'Tipcat', played with a stick and a bat, was accompanied by music played on fiddles. This may later have given rise to the 'Hey Diddle Diddle, the Cat and the Fiddle' rhyme in the sixteenth century.

Le Catt Cum Le Fiddle: a London tavern in Bucklersbury (1501); renamed The Catte and the Fiddle. (1536–1660)

Catt and Fiddle: a London tavern in St Lucknors Lane. (1663)

Catt and Fiddle: a London tavern in Fleet Street. (1568–1660s)

Catt and Kittens: a London tavern near Eastcheap. (1823)
Cat and Lion: an inn at Stockport. (Before 1866). The name is explained by the following lines: 'The lion is strong, the cat is vicious, My ale is strong, and so is my liquors.'
Cat and Wheel: a pub at Castle Green, Bristol. (1866)
Cat Head: village inn at Chiselborough, Somerset. (today)
Cats Head: a London tavern in Orchard Street, Stable Yard, Westminster. (Before 1761)
Catt: a London tavern in Old Fish Street. (1633–34)

Catt: a London tavern in Salisbury Court. (1648–60s)
Salutation and Cat: a London tavern in Newgate Street. (1744–71; 1794)
This name sometimes appears elsewhere as the Cat and Salutation. It originates from the idea that a cat was present at the moment when the angel Gabriel greeted Mary with the news that she was to bear Christ. This greeting was known as the 'Angelic Salutation'.
Whitingtons Cat: a London tavern in Long Lane, West Smithfield. (1657)
Whittingtons Cat: a London tavern in Church Row, Bethnal Green. (1826–27)
Whittington & Cat: a London tavern at 35 High Street, Whitechapel. (1809–27)
Whittingtons & Cat: a London tavern in Golden Lane. (1668)

With modern British pubs cats are more popular. According to Janice Anderson, recent examples with feline names include the following:
Black Cat; Cat and Cracker; Cat and Custard Pot; Cat and Mustard Pot; Cat and Lion; Cat and Mutton; Cat and Tiger; Cat's Whiskers; Cat in the Basket; Cat in the Cage; Cat in the Wall; Cat in the Well; Cat in the Window; Civet Cat; Ginger Tom; Laughing Cat; Mad Cat; Old Cat; Poplar Kitten; ; Rampant Cat; Red Cat; Romping Cat; Salutation and Cat; Squinting Cat; Tabby Cat.

According to Geraldine Mellor, there is also a pub called the Burmese Cat at Melton Mowbray in Leicestershire, and one called the Cheshire Cat at Ellesmere Port in Cheshire. In France there is a Hunchback Cat at Lille and a White Cat (*Chatte Blanche*) at Lyons.

Bibliography
1987. Anderson, J. *Cat-a-logue*. Guinness Books, Enfield, Middlesex.
1866. Larwood, J and Hotten, J C. *The History of Signboards*. Hotten, London.
1972. Lillywhite, B. *London Signs*. Allen and Unwin, London.
1988. Mellor, G. 'At the Sign of the Cat'. In: *Cat World Annual* 1988.

CAT PHOTOGRAPHY

Many famous photographers have sought to catch the moods and actions of cats and a few of them have become feline specialists, among them:

In England: Jane Burton, Paddy Cutts, Toby Glanville, Marc Henrie.

In France: Yann Arthus-Bertrand, Jean-Michel Labat.

In America: Bill Hayward ('If you really want to know people, ask them about their cats.') and Terry Gruber ('I was up to my ears in cats – my camera began to develop hairballs.').

In Japan: Tetsu Yamazaki.

Bibliography

1958. Spies, J. *Cats and How I Photograph Them*. New York.

1978. Hayward, B. *Cat People*. Doubleday, New York.

1979. Gruber, T. *Working Cats*. Lippincott, New York.

1987. Suarès, J.C. *The Photographed Cat*. Doubleday, New York.

1988. Sturgis, M and Glanville, T. *The English Cat at Home*. Chatto and Windus, London.

1990. Eauclaire, S. *The Cat in Photography*. Little, Brown, Boston.

1992. Coppé, P. *1001 Images of Cats*. Tiger Books International, London.

1992. Gebhardt, R H, Bannon, J and Yamazaki, T. *The Allure of the Cat*. TFH, New Jersey.

1992. Suarès, J.C. (Editor) *Black and White Cats*. Collins, San Francisco.

1993. Henrie, M. *Captivating Cats*. Salamander Books, London.

1993. Laruelle, D. *Les Chats de Yann Arthus-Bertrand*. Editions du Chêne, Paris.

MRS LANGTON'S CATS

In the years between the two World Wars, Gloucester-born Blanche Langton began to assemble an outstanding collection of carved and modelled cats, from sources in both Europe and the Orient. With her husband, Neville Langton, she also made special collecting trips to Egypt, to seek out some more ancient examples. She called these older feline figures her 'BC cats', and her later ones her 'AD cats'.

She continued to add to her collection, known affectionately as 'Mrs Langton's Cats', for over half a century, endlessly searching antique markets, galleries and salerooms for exciting new specimens.

She found Meissen, Staffordshire, Worcester, Rockingham and Lowestoft ceramic cats, Chinese Jade and Japanese Netsuke, selecting each piece with an expert eye. Just before her death in 1974, she donated her AD cats (94 of them) to the Castle Museum in Norwich, where the whole collection is on public display. The BC cats – an incomparable collection of 336 ancient Egyptian cats – went to London University's Petrie Museum in Gower Street. Illustrated catalogues of both collections have been published.

PICASSO'S CATS

In the early part of his career, according to the diaries of his mistress, Fernande Olivier, Pablo Picasso (1881–1973), the Spanish artist, owned two cats, a dog and a monkey. A photograph shows that at least one of these cats was a Siamese.

He observed many cats during his long life and on a number of occasions incorporated them into his paintings. They were usually portrayed in a predatory role and it was clearly the cat as an independent, stalking hunter, rather than as a soft, purring lap-cat, that fascinated Picasso.

He is quoted as saying: 'I want to make a cat like those true cats that I see crossing the road. They don't have anything in common with house pets; they have bristling fur and run like demons. If they look at you, you would say that they want to jump on your face and scratch your eyes out. The street cat is a real wild animal. And have you ever noticed that female cats – free cats – are always pregnant. Obviously they don't think of anything but making love.'

Bibliography
1995. Cox, N and Povey, D. *A Picasso Bestiary*. Academy Editions, London.

POSTAGE STAMP CATS

Designs for postage stamps have frequently included cats of one kind or another and these have become the subject of thematic collections for many philatelists.

The first cat seen on a stamp was issued back in 1887 by the German State of Bergedorf. It depicts a cat with a fish in its mouth.

The first modern cat stamp dates from 1930. Issued in Spain to commemorate Lindberg's famous transatlantic flight, it shows Charles Lindberg's black cat called Patsy. She accompanied him during the first leg of his epic journey, from San Diego to New York. Since then 115 different countries have issued stamps showing domestic cats of one kind or another.

The first set of stamps devoted exclusively to cats was offered by Poland in 1964. Since then, special sets of feline stamps showing various breeds of cats have been issued by many other countries including Albania, Bulgaria, Equatorial Guinea, Fujeira (Trucial States), Great Britain, Guinea-Bissau, Guyana, Jersey, Kampuchea, Korea, Manama, Marshall Islands, Moçambique, Mongolia, Nicaragua, Oman, Romania, St Vincent, Sharjah, USA and Vietnam.

There is now a specialist organization devoted to this subject: the 'Cats on Stamps Study Unit' (1300 Crescent Drive, Elizabeth City, NC 27909, USA) that issues a publication called *Cat Mews*.

Bibliography

1951. Way and Standen. *Zoology in Postage Stamps*.

1977. James, A (Editor). *The Stanyon Book of Cats*. Random House, New York (illustrated with cat stamps).

1980. Ladd, F and Ladd, N. *Illustrated Cat Stamp Checklist*.

1994. Schuessler, R. 'Cats on Stamps'. In: *Cat World* Magazine, February 1994. p.28–29.

SEARLE'S CATS

British artist, Ronald Searle (1920–), created a collection of delightfully rotund, hairy cats in a long series of humorous cartoons which were eventually collected together in book form.

Bibliography

1969. Searle, R. *Searle's Cats*. Dobson Books, London.

STEINLEN'S CATS

The cats sketched by the French artist Théophile Steinlen (1859–1923) are not cartoon cats, although they are often presented

in a series of images similar to those of a strip cartoon. But the individual cats are true felines. Their adventures are those of cats, not caricatured humans. In a classic example, a cat sees a snowman standing outside the house. With the typical feline greeting gesture, the cat rubs up against the legs of the snowman. The heat of the cat's body melts the snowman's leg and it falls on top of the startled cat.

A Siamese cat, drawn by Theophile Steinlen

Bibliography

1933. Steinlein, T. *Cats and other Animals.*

ND. Steinlein, T. *Des Chats; Images sans paroles.* Flammarion, Paris. (Facsimile edition published by Libro in 1981.)

LOUIS WAIN'S CATS

Louis Wain (1860–1939) was a prolific British illustrator whose anthropomorphic portrayals of cats made him the most easily recognized of all feline artists. His strict upbringing in a Victorian family (he was described as a sickly child with a hare-lip) resulted in a quiet, delayed rebellion that, in his adult life, took the form of a sentimental, infantile sense of humour. It was the intensity of this humour that gave his cloyingly sweet pictures their undeniable strength. It was as though, when he put pen to paper, he was able to unleash his own, hitherto suppressed childhood.

His marriage was a disaster. His family disapproved of his wife and she became bedridden, dying after only three years. During her illness their only pleasure stemmed from a black and white kitten called Peter and it was this animal that Louis Wain began to sketch. From these sketches he began to develop a personal style which, in 1886, led to his first illustrated book, *Madame Tabby's Establishment*. It was the start of four decades of high output of both book illustrations and postcards.

In 1890 he was invited to become the second President of the National Cat Club, following the resignation of Harrison Weir. His popularity was enormous in the early part of the twentieth century. In 1925 H G Wells said of Wain in a radio broadcast: 'he has made the cat his own. He invented a cat style, a cat society, a whole cat world.'

His career ended tragically, his last fourteen years being spent in asylums. In 1914 he had been thrown off the top of a horse-drawn bus and was badly concussed. The accident seemed to affect his brain and in the early 1920s he became paranoid and eventually violent, attacking his sisters without reason. In 1924 he was certified insane and admitted to a pauper ward in the Middlesex County Mental Asylum, suffering from schizophrenia. Thanks to the intervention of the prime minister, in 1925 he was moved to Bethlehem Royal Hospital. In 1930 he was moved again, this time to the mental hospital at Napsbury near St Albans and he remained there until his death in 1939. During his final years he continued to draw cats but now, in his confused state, they were transformed into little more than fantastic patterns.

The National Cat Club badge designed by Louis Wain

Bibliography

1917. Shaw, J F. *In 'Louis Wain' Land*.

1968. Dale, R. *Louis Wain, the Man who Drew Cats*. William Kimber, London. (Enlarged edition in 1991.)

1972. Reade, B. *Louis Wain*. Victoria and Albert Museum, London. (Exhibition catalogue.)

1977. Dale, R. *Catland*. Duckworth, London.

1982. Silvester, J and Mobbs, A. *The Cat Fancier*. Longman, London.

1983. Parkin, M. *Louis Wain's Edwardian Cats*. London.

1982. Latimer, H. *Louis Wain. King of the Cat Artists*. Papyrus, New York.

Note: Claire Necker also lists no fewer than eighty-seven books illustrated by Wain.

*A poster for an American cat
show in 1883*

13

SHOW CATS

THE MOST SPECTACULAR and most celebrated domestic cats in the world are undoubtedly those that take the prizes at the major cat shows. These are the stars of the feline world, carefully bred and immaculately groomed for the occasion. For moggie lovers they may seem to be almost too pampered, too perfected, too extreme in their refinement, but the high standards they achieve help to elevate felines from mere alley cats to revered super-cats.

The first cat show took place in Winchester, in southern England, in the year 1598. It was no more than a sideshow at the annual St Giles Fair, but it was nevertheless a competitive event, since it is recorded that prizes were given for the best ratter and the best mouser.

Similar small shows were staged at similar fairs, but these were of little significance and had no official status. The breeding of pedigreed cats had little meaning at this time.

In was not until the second half of the last century that serious, competitive cat showing was staged. The earliest example was at a London house in 1861, but this was still not a true public exhibition.

In the 1860s, minor cat shows were held in both England and the United States. In America there had already been annual livestock shows for many years. In New England, these started in earnest in 1832 and by the 1860s it is thought they must have included cat competitions because, by the 1870s, the Maine Coon, for example, was already considered as a separate and established breed for competition.

The first major cat show in the world took place on Thursday, 13th July 1871 at the Crystal Palace in London. It was organized by a well-known animal artist of the day, Harrison Weir. There were so many visitors that the cats themselves were barely visible in the dense throng. Weir was amazed by the public response. On the journey to the Crystal Palace he had serious doubts about the wisdom of his plan, fearing the animals would 'sulk or cry for liberty'. But when he arrived he found them lying peacefully on crimson cushions. There was no noise except for widespread purring and gentle lapping of fresh milk.

Looking at the exhibits at the first cat show

A total of 170 cats were entered, although the prize money amounted to less than £10 ($18) for the whole competition. One of the prize-winners was Harrison Weir's own fourteen-year-old tabby called The Old Lady, which is not surprising when one discovers that two of the three judges were Weir's brother and Weir himself.

If this system of judging left something to be desired, it must be recorded that, thanks to Harrison Weir, cats were, for the very first time, given specific standards and classes. These form the basis of the system still employed at modern cat shows all over the world.

This first cat major cat show was so successful that a second one was staged later in the same year and, although it was only open for one day, it attracted 19,310 visitors. Two more shows were held in the following year, after which it became an annual event. The enormous popularity of these cat shows saw the idea spread rapidly to other cities in the British Isles and eventually around the world.

In 1887 the National Cat Club was formed to rule this new competitive world. The president was, needless to say, Harrison Weir. By 1893 the first official cat stud book had been started, and pedigree cat breeding had begun in earnest.

The first major American cat shows also took place in the 1870s. As early as 1878, for instance, there was a six-day National Cat Show in Boston. During that decade there were others in most of the Eastern cities, and as far west as Chicago. Later, in 1895, the biggest of all these early American shows was held at Madison Square Gardens in New York. It was organized by an Englishman, Mr J Hyde, and attracted 176 entries. Due to its success, other shows quickly followed and were soon established as annual fixtures.

Today there are no fewer than sixty-five annual shows in Britain and 400 in the United States. Unfortunately, the world of cat show organizers has become increasingly competitive within its ranks, and there have been splits and divisions since the earliest days. The result is that there is no single authority in either Great Britain or the United States, and each club or society has its own slightly different rules and classes. All of this can be confusing to the outsider, but for the cats it does not make a great deal of difference. The survival of pedigree competition is the important thing, maintaining the serious attitude toward pure-bred felines and preventing cats from losing status in twentieth-century society.

With more than 94 per cent of cats today being non-pedigree, the cats of the show world constitute only a tiny minority of the general feline population, but this does not matter. As long as the elite pedigrees exist to be photographed and exhibited, they will transmit an aura of importance to domestic cats in general. They are the ambassadors of the feline world, and when over 2,000 of them gather each December for the biggest cat show in the world – the National Cat Show in London – the interest they arouse is an admirable advertisement for the value we place on our feline companions.

BREED POPULARITY

The most popular cats have always been the moggies, the non-pedigrees, the ordinary house pets. They are the rough, tough survivors whose parents have somehow managed to avoid being neutered by kindly feline welfare workers. Despite endless trips to the vet for 'altering' sessions, moggies are still the most common and the most widespread of all kinds of cats today, right across the globe. Their tenacity and their ability to infiltrate their way into the homes and the hearts of the public is second to none. Pedigree cats are everywhere rare by comparison.

But among those pure-bred individuals, which are the most popular breeds? In the very beginning, in the cat shows of the Victorian era, it was the short-haired cats (the aristocratic cousins of the moggies) that were originally the most favoured. Then, the long-haired cats arrived, the Angoras and the Persians, and they quickly rose to dominate the exhibition scene. The Angoras were soon swamped out by the Persians, who were then joined by the exotic Siamese. As the years passed, more and more breeds were introduced, each finding followers and fanatical supporters. Today a pedigree cat

A Russian long-hair cat, by Harrison Weir in 1889

show is fascinatingly complex, with new breeds appearing each year and with new colours of old breeds being developed. But which, today, are the 'top cats'? After all the changes that have occurred in over a century of pedigree cat exhibitions, which are the breeds that have finally won through to become the most popular pedigree breeds today?

The best way to find out is to check the number of registrations for each breed at one of the major cat societies. One of the biggest registration organizations in the world is the CFA (The Cat Fanciers Association), and here are the 'top ten' breeds, as reflected by their recent registration records:

		Percentage
1	Persian	79.4
2	Siamese	5.5
3	Abyssinian	3.6
4	Maine Coon	2.8
5	Burmese	1.9
6	Oriental Shorthair	1.6
7	American Shorthair	1.6
8	Exotic Shorthair	1.3
9	Scottish Fold	1.2
10	Colourpoint Shorthair	1.1

14

MYSTERY CATS

BRITISH BIG CAT

Modern folklore has created its own legends, from flying saucers to crop circles, to replace the obsolete angels and ghouls of the past. Fairies have become aliens, as the supernatural has kept pace with modern technology. In animal folklore there has been a similar shift. The dragons and unicorns of yesterday required a modern, believable equivalent and it was found in the form of the 'mystery cat'. As recently as 1983 it was claimed that, even in over-populated and over-explored Britain: 'a large, unidentified carnivore is quietly living in our countryside, a living fossil, waiting to be discovered and classified.'

Given the name of the 'British Big Cat', from the 1960s onwards it became the subject of countless newspaper articles and several books. The phenomenon embraced the following dramatic sightings: The Shooter's Hill Cheetah (1963); The Surrey Puma (362 sightings between 1964 and 1966); The Nottingham Lioness (1976); The Glenfarg Lynx (1976); The Cannich Puma (1979); The Powys Beast (1980); The Beast of Exmoor (1983); The Kellas Cat (1984).

There are three plausible explanations for these sightings:

1 In the boom period of the 1960s many small zoos opened in Britain. Some were well run, but many were amateurish. Captive bred pumas were a glut on the market at the time, thanks to repeated breeding successes at London Zoo and elsewhere. As a result, quite a large number of pumas found their way into these new and often imperfectly secured menageries. Some even found their way into private hands as exotic pets. It is highly likely that some of these escaped from their flimsy enclosures. Wishing to avoid criticism, the zoo owners simply kept quiet about these incidents. This would certainly explain the Surrey Puma sightings. Other exotic cat escapes could also explain most of the other sightings listed above.

2   In 1976, the Dangerous Wild Animals Act was passed in the UK, which meant that anyone owning a large cat, whether in a zoo or as a pet, required a licence. The licences in question were extremely expensive and difficult to obtain, with the result that many desperate owners of large cats probably reacted by simply turning them loose in the British countryside. This would account for the sudden increase in sightings in the late 1970s and the 1980s.

3   The Kellas Cat, and other similar sightings of a more modest feline, little bigger than a British wild cat, were originally thought to be evidence of another 'mystery cat' species, but the animals involved are now thought to be hybrids between feral black domestic cats and British wild cats.

Cases where the 'British Big Cat' is supposed to have savaged various farm animals are in most cases probably due to attacks by dogs. The killing methods of cats and dogs are quite different and the wounds inflicted in these instances seldom match with feline predatory techniques.

Bibliography
1974. Dent, A. *Lost Beasts of Britain*. Harrap, London.
1983. Francis, D. *Cat Country: The Quest for the British Big Cat*. David and Charles, Newton Abbot, Devon.
1984. Beer, T. *The Beast of Exmoor*. Countryside Productions, Barnstaple.
1986. McEwan, G. *Mystery Animals of Britain and Ireland*. Robert Hale, London.
1989. Shuker, K. *Mystery Cats of the World*. Robert Hale, London.
1993. Francis, D. *The Beast of Exmoor*. Jonathan Cape, London.
1993. Francis, D. *My Highland Kellas Cats*. Jonathan Cape, London.

CHERRY-COLOURED CAT

The search for a genuine, bright red cat has always fascinated cat lovers, so when the famous American showman Phineas Barnun proudly announced that he had acquired such an animal and was about to put it on display, excited crowds flocked to see it. After paying their money, they found themselves staring at an ordinary black cat. Angry at being deceived they demanded their money back, but were bluntly refused by Barnum who reminded them, truthfully, that some cherries are indeed black.

HARIMAU JALOR

In the Malaysian state of Trengganu, the local people speak of a giant tiger with horizontal stripes instead of the usual vertical ones. They call it the Harimau Jalor and repeatedly tell of its existence, but since there is no living or dead specimen to support their stories, their reports have been ignored and the animal is still considered to be an imaginative fiction rather than a scientific fact.

HONG KONG CAT

In 1976 more than twenty dogs were slaughtered by an unknown feline in the New Territories of Hong Kong. According to local villagers it was four feet long and had blackish-grey fur and a long tail. Its identity was never established.

IKIMIZI

In Rwanda the local people speak of a mystery cat they call the Ikimizi, which looks like a cross between a leopard and a lion. It is said to have a spotted grey coat and a beard under the chin.

Although hybrids have been created between leopards and lions (and called leopons) in the artificial confines of zoos, there is no authenticated record of such a hybrid occurring naturally where the two species co-exist in the wild. It is therefore highly unlikely that the Ikimizi really exists.

However, it must be admitted that the presence of such an unusal animal is firmly believed in a number of quite separate cultures in tropical Africa. In the Cameroons, it is known as the Bung

Bung; in Ethiopia it is called the Abasambo; in the Central African Republic is goes by the name of Bakanga; and in Uganda it is the Ntarargo.

Taken together, these local names suggest that there is perhaps, after all, something to be explained. The answer may lie in the direction of the Spotted Lion. This is known to exist, if only from a few skins, and only as a freak mutant. Local people, seeing a Spotted Lion, might naturally assume that it was a cross between a leopard and a lion, rather than an adult lion that had failed to lose its juvenile spotting (although this latter explanation makes much more sense scientifically).

JAGUARETE

The early naturalists, Buffon and Bewick, both refer to this mysterious animal, which they also called the 'couguar noir' or 'Black tiger'. They describe it as follows:

It has a dusky coat, sometimes with black spots, but usually plain. The undersides are pale and the upper lip and paws are white. It has sharply pointed ears. A large, powerful cat, it is 'cruel and fierce' and much feared by the local people. Frequenting the sea-shore, it feeds on turtles' eggs. It also takes large reptiles and fish. Its hunting methods are remarkable: 'In order to catch the alligator, they lie down on their belly at the edge of the river, strike the water to make a noise, and as soon as the alligator raises its head above the water, dart their claws into its eyes and drag it on shore.'

It would seem from this description that the animal in question is no more than a melanistic jaguar or puma; possibly both, confused and amalgamated in local stories. But its pale underparts and white paws do not fit with this explanation, as melanistic cats tend to be black all over.

The plot thickens with the comment by another early naturalist, Thomas Pennant, that two jaguaretes were actually exhibited in London in the eighteenth century. Precisely what they were remains a mystery at present, but the most likely explanation is that they were some kind of mutant jaguar.

KELLAS CAT

The Kellas Cat is a melanistic hybrid between feral black domestic cats and Scottish Wildcats. In the 1980s there were a number of reports of a wild-living, long-legged, black cat in Scotland, in the region east of Inverness. In the mid-1980s, specimens were obtained from near the hamlet of Kellas and some of these were examined at the Natural History Museum in London. The animal is slightly larger than a domestic cat and less stocky than a Scottish wild cat. Its presence gave rise to the romantic suggestion that there was an unknown, wild member of the cat family roaming the more remote parts of Scotland.

Four rival suggestions were put forward regarding this cat:

1 A new species of wild cat.
2 A feral domestic black cat.
3 A melanistic Scottish wild cat (*Felis sylvestris*)
4 A hybrid between a feral domestic black cat and a Scottish wild cat.

Anatomical measurements of the few Kellas Cat specimens known support the fourth suggestion. In all but one case, they show

An historical illustration of Felis sylvestris

certain features of domestic cats and others of wild cats. Their impressive size is doubtless due to hybrid vigour. In a single, exceptional case, the measurements match those of the wild cat, suggesting that, in addition to the hybrids, there exists the occasional melanistic Scottish wild cat.

The presence of these Kellas Cats may explain the tales of a fairy cat called the *cait sith* in Scottish Highland folklore (See Chapter 4, Legendary Cats.)

Bibliography
1989. Shuker, K. *Mystery Cats of the World*. Robert Hale, London.
1993. Francis, D. *My Highland Kellas Cats*. Jonathan Cape, London.

MADAGASCAR CAT

In 1939 there was a French report of a giant, cave-dwelling cat rather like a lion, that inhabited remote, unexplored areas of the island of Madagascar. It was romantically suggested that this represented a remnant population of sabre-toothed felines. The report was published by Paul Cazard in *Le Chasseur Français*. He suggested the mounting of an expedition to search for this unknown cat, but no action was ever taken and the Madagascar sabre-tooth must remain in the mystic realms of the mystery cat.

MITLA

The explorer Colonel Percy Fawcett wrote of his observations in the Bolivian forests: 'In the forests were various beasts still unfamiliar to zoologists, such as the Mitla, which I have seen twice, a black dog-like cat about the size of a foxhound.'

There is no such cat known to science and it was later suggested that what Fawcett had seen was in fact the rather strange-looking South American Bush Dog (*Speothos*). Karl Shuker, in his scholarly study, *Mystery Cats of the World*, has offered an alternative candidate, namely the little-known Small-eared Dog (*Atelocynus*), which he points out moves in a rather feline way, with graceful actions that are not typically dog-like. Ultimately, as he says, the 'dog-like cat' may prove to be no more than an already identified 'cat-like dog'.

MNGWA

In the coastal forests of Tanzania, a huge, grey-striped cat known locally as the Mngwa or Nunda, and which has apparently been featured in African native songs for over 800 years, is still believed by some to be surviving in remote corners. Because of its night-time attacks on humans it is widely feared.

Various identities have been suggested, including a giant version of the African Golden Cat (*Felis aurata*), but there is no scientific evidence to support this or any other zoological explanation. This may, in fact, be just another savage legendary cat invented to explain the violent nocturnal deaths of human rivals.

MOUNTAIN TIGER

In northern Chad, the local people speak of a *tigre de montaigne* which is described as being larger than a lion, having a terrifying roar, being cave-dwelling, having red fur banded with white stripes, no tail, large hairy feet and teeth that protrude from its mouth. It is said to hunt large antelope.

In the south-west of Chad a similar beast is known as the *hadjel*. In the Central African Republic it is called the *coq-ninji*, the *gassingram* or the *vassoko*. The romantic view is that these creatures could perhaps represent a surviving remnant population of the sabre-toothed tiger. Although this is so unlikely as to be hardly worth considering, it is nevertheless difficult to guess what could have inspired such a widespread legend.

ONZA

It has long been claimed that a large cat exists in Mexico that is neither a puma nor a jaguar. Locals have named this animal the *onza* and describe it as a 'cheetah-like puma'. It is said to be similar to a puma except for the following features: there are horizontal stripes on the insides of the front legs; the body is much more slender; the legs are longer and stronger; the claws are non-retractile; the paws are narrower and more elongated.

The animal is said to be confined to the Sierra Madre Occidentale mountains in Mexico, only rarely descending to the lowlands. It lives in regions that are impassable to vehicles and difficult even for horses. This is said to explain the fact that it has gone largely undetected, even in modern times. It is reputed to hunt deer as its main form of prey.

A female *onza* was shot by a deer-hunter in 1986 and a detailed examination of its body revealed an animal that was 186cm (6ft 1in) long, of which 73cm (29in) was tail. Its weight was 27kg (60lb). A colour photograph of the carcass shows a skinny animal that looks like an emaciated, sub-adult puma in very poor condition. The leg-stripes are not at all clear and the claws on the front feet appear to be sheathed. The protruding claws on the hind paws appear to have been added to the photograph in ink. However, it does have rather long, pointed ears for a typical puma and its dissection did prove that, although it was extremely slender, it was not starving or abnormally emaciated, despite its superficial appearance.

On the strength of this evidence, it seems likely that the *onza* is, at best, an unusual, slender-bodied race of the ordinary puma, but not a separate species. The biggest drawback to its credibility is that all its specializations point towards a cheetah-like way of life – hunting on open plains – where the lanky, long-limbed body would be at such an advantage in high-speed pursuits of fleet-footed prey. Yet, the *onza* lives in difficult mountain terrain, precisely the wrong type of habitat for an animal with that kind of build. For the moment therefore, despite the existence of a carcass, the *onza* must remain firmly on the list of mystery cats.

Bibliography
1961. Marshall, R. *The Onza*. Exposition Press, New York.

Red Tiger

White tigers are no longer a mystery. These pallid mutants exist and have been exhibited and bred in a number of zoos. But there was also a report in 1936 of a plain red tiger – one with the usual background colour but no stripes. This uniformly reddish-brown animal was said to inhabit a region of open sandy tracts, where it was thought that its plain colour would act as better camouflage. Its existence, however, has never been scientifically verified.

Ruffed Cat

In 1940 the zoologist Ivan Sanderson was travelling in the mountains of north-west Mexico when he came across the skin of a very strange cat, which was being offered for sale by local trappers. The head and body measured 180cm (71in) and the comparatively short tail another 45cm (17.5in). It was clear from the pelt that the animal had a short face, long legs and big paws. The brown fur had wavy stripes on the flanks and upper legs. The tail and lower legs were a darker brown than the rest. Amazingly, this cat also had a large ruff of fur around its neck.

In great excitement, he bought the pelt of what appeared to him to be a new species of large feline, but before he could return home it was lost in a hurricane and flood. He did see another similar skin for sale later, in a market at Colima, but could not, by then, afford the very high price being asked for it.

If his description is accurate, it is clear that this skin did not belong to any previously recognized cat. Although Sanderson was known to his friends as having a rather active imagination, he was too good a zoologist to have imagined all these unusual details. Sadly, Sanderson is now dead and the mystery of his Ruffed Cat remains unresolved.

SANTER

At the end of the nineteenth century a mystery cat called the Santer terrorized the farming communities of North Carolina, killing livestock and causing a flurry of newspaper articles and public statements. It was described as being the size of a large dog, grey in colour, and 'striped from the end of its nose to the end of its tail'. Its true identity was never established and by the end of the century it had vanished, never to reappear.

SIEMEL'S CAT

There is a record from the early part of the twentieth century that the big-game hunter Sacha Siemel, while on an expedition to the Mata Grosso, shot a large cat that he claimed was a cross between a jaguar and a puma. It had the ground colour of a puma but the spots of a jaguar and was very heavily built. For such a hybrid to occur in the wild is so unlikely as to be hardly worth serious consideration, but the identity of the animal remains a mystery.

SPOTTED LION

Since 1903, rumours of spotted cats have filtered through from tropical Africa. To the locals it is known as the Marozi. To science it is looked upon simply as a freak – an occasional oddity of no special interest. Young lions often show distinct spotting of the coat and these spots disappear as the animals become adult, so it would not be particularly surprising if, in one or two isolated cases, this juvenile spotting was late in disappearing.

In the early 1930s two adult spotted lions were shot near a farm in the Aberdares and their heavily spotted skins at last proved beyond any doubt that such animals really did exist. But it was still felt that they were merely isolated genetic freaks.

Despite the lack of scientific interest, and inspired by these skins, a young explorer called Kenneth Dower set off, later in the 1930s, to discover what he thought was an exciting new species. Although he failed in his quest, he bravely wrote a whole book on the subject.

Supporters of the spotted lion have since suggested that it might perhaps be a rare forest race of lions, adapted to the dappled light, where the spots would improve the animal's camouflage. This is reasonable enough in theory, but until hard evidence is available, the animal must continue to be looked upon as a local mutant rather than as a whole new sub-species.

Bibliography
1937. Dower, K C G. *The Spotted Lion*. Heinemann, London.
1989. Shuker, K P N. *Mystery Cats of the World*. Robert Hale, London.

WARACABRA TIGER

The Waracabra Tiger is supposed to be a pack-hunting jaguar whose terrifying, eerie howls are frequently heard echoing through the Guyanan forest in the dead of night. These howls sound like the cries of the trumpeter bird (known locally as the waracabra bird), hence the name of the 'tiger'.

Unfortunately, although often heard, this mysterious beast is never seen. American zoologist Lee Crandall investigated the phenomenon and came to the conclusion that the pack-hunters in question were, in reality, South American Bush Dogs (*Speothos*), but it has been pointed out that these animals, although they do, indeed, hunt in packs in the forest, do not have such loud, eerie cries.

For this reason, there are those who believe that the waracabra tiger is of considerable interest. What they overlook, of course, is that the packs of wild dogs could easily disturb sleeping trumpeter birds and set off their very loud alarm cries. This combination – of a pack of scurrying mammalian figures in the forest, accompanied by loud, echoing cries – could easily create a legend of a nightmarish, pack-hunting jaguar.

WATER TIGER

The local people in various regions of South America have sinister legends about a *tigre de agua* or water tiger. It is said to be a savage beast capable of dragging a swimming horse down and disembowelling it. Described as a huge cat with powerful claws and fangs – that are sometimes described as so huge as to be 'tusks'.

The water tiger goes by many names in different places: the *yaguaro*, the *yaguaruigh*, the *iemisch*, the *maipolina*, or the 'water mother'. The romantic view is that, in some dark, remote forest, there still lurks a form of sabre-toothed tiger, a relic from prehistoric days. A more realistic view is that the sightings are a confused combination of giant otters, swimming jaguars and even crocodiles.

WINGED CAT

In his study *Animal Fakes and Frauds*, Peter Dance reports on a mysterious (stuffed) winged cat which was offered for sale in the early 1960s. Information on the amazing animal was distributed from an address in Bond Street, London.

It dated back to the nineteenth century, when it was claimed that the wings had started to grow when the cat was very young. At some time while it was alive a circus owner exhibited it, but its original owner demanded its return and there was a lawsuit about legal ownership. The original owner won his case and the cat was shipped back to him. It was dead on arrival and there were claims that its food for the journey had been deliberately poisoned. The animal was sent to a taxidermist, stuffed and placed in a mahogany and glass case. After many years it ended up gathering dust in an attic. It had now been rescued and was being offered for sale. However, offers by Peter Dance to buy it remained unanswered.

This is not the only report of a winged cat. Another dates from 1899. The animal in question, a tabby, lived in England at the village of Wivelscombe in Somerset and had two fur-covered flanges protruding from its back which flapped about when the cat ran. A photograph of it appeared in the November 1899 issue of *Strand* magazine and caused a minor sensation.

A third example is said to have been exhibited in the 1930s at the Oxford Zoo (which closed down in 1939). A fourth was exhibited at Blackpool museum. Further cases have been reported from the United States and Sweden. The Swedish winged cat was shot in 1949 and carefully examined. Its 'wing-span' was said to be 23in (58cm) and it weighed 20lb (9kg).

There are three possible explanations for these freak animals. Either all these cats together represent a widespread deception – a faking tradition that keeps resurfacing – or they indicate the existence of a strange mutation that occurs spontaneously from time to time, or they suggest some sort of recurrent congenital deformity. The most likely explanation would seem to be a rare mutation, but without a specimen to examine scientifically, the case remains open.

Bibliography
1976. Dance, P. *Animal Fakes and Frauds*. Sampson Low, Maidenhead.
1986. Brandreth, G. *Cats' Tales*. Robson Books, London.

WOBO

According to the local people in remote parts of Ethiopia, when encountered by Victorian explorers, there existed in that country a huge cat, called a *wobo*, which was bigger than a lion and which had dark stripes. It was also referred to as the Mendelit and, in neighbouring Sudan, as the Abu Sotan. There were specific claims that a pelt existed and had been seen by many people. The most likely explanation is that the pelt was of an imported tiger-skin and that vivid imaginations related this skin to nocturnal, dimly observed sightings of lions or striped hyenas, to create in the mind a monstrous 'African Tiger'.

15

TALISMAN CATS

BECKONING CAT

The image of a cat with one paw raised in a beckoning movement is a popular Japanese talisman or lucky charm. It is known as the *maneki-neko*. If worn on the body it brings good luck and also wards off bad luck. Images of beckoning cats tied around the waist are said to protect the wearer from pain and ill-health. If placed at the entrance of a building, a beckoning cat made of clay, wood, or papier-mâché protects the occupants in a similar way. In the absence of an image, even the written symbol for the cat is alone considered to have protective value.

The legend of the origin of the beckoning cat is as follows: The temple at Gotoku-ji was a very poor one. Although the monks were starving, they shared their food with their pet cat. One day the cat was sitting by the side of the road outside the temple, when a group of rich Samurai rode up. The cat beckoned to them and they followed it into the temple. Once inside, heavy rain forced them to shelter there and they passed the time learning about the Buddhist philosophy. Later, one of the Samurai returned to take religious instruction and eventually endowed the temple with a large estate. His family were buried there and near their tombs a small cat-shrine was built to the memory of the beckoning cat.

A popular embellishment of the legend adds a more dramatic moment to the Samurai incident. When the terrible rainstorm arrived it brought lightning with it. A bolt of lightning struck the ground exactly where the Samurai had been standing, just before they followed the cat into the temple. The cat therefore saved their lives, for which they were immensely grateful.

Although this sounds like a fanciful tale, it may actually have happened. When a thunderstorm is approaching it causes electro-magnetic disturbances and it is now known that these changes can upset cats. Their reaction to this magnetic interference is to start grooming themselves nervously. When doing this, they begin by bringing up a paw to wash their face, and this action looks very like a beckoning gesture. So, if the Samurai paused at the temple just as a thunderstorm was approaching, they may well have seen the cat starting to groom itself and misinterpreted this as an urgent beckon, encouraging them to enter the temple. By responding to it, they would have avoided being hit by lightning, so that whole legend may, after all, have a scientific basis.

Today the temple has been swallowed up by the western suburbs of Tokyo, but it remains a popular centre for those who wish to pray for their cats, and the cat-shrine is regularly festooned with offerings. It is also believed that if you buy an effigy of the beckoning cat and place it among the many others already displayed at the temple, your most urgent desire will be fulfilled. Students, for example, sometimes buy a cat-offering when they are facing a difficult examination. The effigies are on sale at the temple and it is possible to buy very small ones (for small wishes) right up to full cat-sized ones (for big wishes).

The cat breed known as the Japanese Bobtail is now closely identified with the legendary Beckoning Cat, and it is thought that to own one will bring good luck.

Some authors record a completely different legend to explain the popularity of the Beckoning Cat. According to this tale, a famous woman in Yoshiwara was about to be attacked by a dangerous snake. Her favourite cat saw the danger and tried to warn her, but was killed in the attempt. She had an effigy of this cat carved in wood, to commemorate its brave deed, and copies of this became popular as lucky charms, to protect their owners from danger.

KASPAR

A black cat carved in wood, Kaspar is the famous 'lucky cat' employed by the Savoy Hotel in London to occupy the fourteenth seat at dinner parties when the guests unexpectedly form a group of 'unlucky thirteen'. For some people, the superstition about not sitting down to dinner as a member of a party of thirteen is held so strongly that it can create something of a crisis for a top restaurant. The Savoy suavely solves the problem by ceremoniously placing the figure of Kaspar in an extra chair. The wooden cat, carved by Basil Ionides in 1926, has been used by many famous guests including, on several occasions, that great cat lover Sir Winston Churchill.

In origin, the fear of the number thirteen dates back to Norse mythology when twelve gods were joined at a feast by an evil spirit, who caused havoc. Later, the idea of 'unlucky thirteen' was taken up by Christian mythology and given a new boost by the number of guests present at The Last Supper.

In the case of the Savoy Hotel, this superstition had acquired extra significance when one of its guests, who had been forced to sit down as host of a party of thirteen because one of his guests cancelled at the last moment, was later shot dead in his office. After that, the hotel always provided a member of their staff if an extra place was needed to avoid a group of thirteen. However, some dinner parties involved confidential conversations, and so Kaspar was born as a 'silent fourteenth'. When he was placed at the table, a napkin was tied around his neck and waiters were always careful to change his place settings for each course of the meal.

RUTTERKIN

By definition a talisman is a charm that brings good luck, but it can also be used by its owner specifically to bring bad luck to others. This was allegedly the case with Rutterkin, the reputedly evil black cat (with eyes like burning coal) that was the familiar of the seventeenth century English serving-woman Joan Flower, who was condemned for practising witchcraft. Joan and her two daughters worked for the Earl of Rutland at Belvoir Castle and stood accused of bewitching his family. Both his sons had died and his wife had become barren, probably from quite independent causes, but a scapegoat had to be found and the three 'Belvoir Witches' were accused of causing these calamities with the help of their pet cat, Rutterkin.

The accusation was that the daughters had stolen intimate objects from the Rutlands and given them to their mother who then rubbed them ceremonially over Rutterkin's magical fur, uttering curses. This was supposedly done with the glove of the eldest son, who then promptly died; then the glove of the younger son, who also died; then with feathers from the bed of the Earl's wife, who subsequently became barren.

Joan Flower's two daughters were hanged for these crimes in 1617 and Joan herself, still protesting her innocence, mysteriously choked on some food and died in prison before she could be executed. Nothing is recorded concerning the fate of Rutterkin himself, although it seems unlikely that he survived the Earl's vengeful persecution of the Flower household.

The three women of the Flower family, from a seventeenth-century pamphlet recording the story

SHASTA

Shasta, a cougar or puma, imported from Mexico, was the living mascot of the University of Houston's football team, who were known as the Cougars. Shasta was retired in 1963, to be replaced by a younger animal.

SILKWORM CAT

Images of cats were placed on the walls of the houses of Chinese silk-worm breeders to protect their silkworms from harm during the breeding season. It was believed that these pictures would have the power to frighten off the rats that often plagued the farmers. Some, more practical farmers also collected together as many live cats as they could to carry out the task, at the most sensitive time of the year.

16

FELINE SAYINGS

CAT-IN-HELL'S CHANCE

The meaning of this phrase (he doesn't have a cat-in-hell's chance = he has no chance at all) is well known, but its origin is not. It is an abbreviation of the phrase 'No more chance than a cat in hell without claws.' It was originally a reference to being in a fight without adequate weapons.

LET THE CAT OUT OF THE BAG

The origin of this phrase, meaning 'to give away a secret', dates back to the eighteenth century when it referred to a market-day trick. Piglets were often taken to market in a small sack, or bag, to be sold. The trickster would put a cat in a bag and pretend that it was a pig. If the buyer insisted on seeing it, he would be told that it was too lively to risk opening up the bag, as the animal might escape. If the cat struggled so much that the trickster let the cat out of the bag, his secret was exposed. A popular name for the bag itself was a 'poke', hence that other expression 'never buy a pig in a poke'.

NINE LIVES

The phrase 'a cat has nine lives' is well known but few people know its origin. It is obviously based on the fact that the cat is unusually resilient, but that does not explain the nine lives. The answer comes from early religious beliefs, where a 'trinity of trinities' was thought to be especially lucky, and therefore ideally suited for the 'lucky' cat.

RAINING CATS AND DOGS

This phrase became popular several centuries ago at a time when the streets of towns and cities were narrow, filthy and had poor drainage. Unusually heavy storms produced torrential flooding which drowned large numbers of the half-starved cats and dogs that foraged there. After a downpour was over, people would emerge to find the corpses of the unfortunate animals, and the more gullible among them believed that the bodies must have fallen from the sky – and that it had literally been raining cats and dogs.

A description of the impact of a severe city storm, written by Jonathan Swift in 1710, supports this view: 'Now from all parts the swelling kennels flow, and bear their trophies with them as they go… drowned puppies, stinking sprats, all drenched in mud, dead cats, and turnip tops, come tumbling down the flood.'

Some classicists prefer a more ancient explanation, suggesting that the phrase is derived from the Greek word for a waterfall: *catadupa*. If rain fell in torrents – like a waterfall – then the saying 'raining *catadupa*' could gradually have become converted into 'raining cats and dogs'.

PROVERBS

There are many proverbs referring to cats. The following are the best known ones. They are arranged in the order in which they were first recorded:

One day as a tiger is worth a thousand years as a sheep.(Ancient)
The cat knows whose lips she licks.(1023)
The cat would eat fish but would not wet her feet. (1225)
As the cat plays with a mouse. (1340)
He is like a cat; fling him which way you will, he'll light on his legs. (1398)
When the cat's away the mice will play. (1470)
Beware of cats that lick from the front and claw from behind. (Fifteenth century)
A cat has nine lives. (1546)
A cat may look at a king. (1546)

All cats are grey in the dark. (1546)
A cat in gloves catches no mice. (1573)
Good liquor will make a cat speak. (1585)
Never was a cat drowned that could see the shore. (1594)
An old cat laps as much milk as a young. (1605)
A muzzled cat was never good mouser. (1605)
The scalded cat fears cold water. (1611)
The cat has kittened in your mouth. (1618)
A baited cat may grow as fierce as a lion. (1620)
As nimble as a blind cat in a barn. (1639)
An old cat sports not with her prey. (1640)
Like a cat on hot bricks. (1678)
The more you rub a cat on the rump, the higher she sets up her tail.
(1678)
Cats eat what hussies spare. (1683)
To put the cat among the pigeons. (1706)
He that plays with cats, must expect to be scratched. (1710)
He who hunts with cats will only catch rats. (1712)

A rat-catcher with his cats

None but cats are allowed to quarrel in my house. (1732)
Cats hide their claws. (1732)
The cat invites the mouse to a feast. (1732)
To let the cat out of the bag. (1760)
Watch which way the cat jumps.(1825)
Enough to make a cat laugh. (1851)
The cat shuts its eyes while it steals cream.(1853)
There are more ways of killing a cat than choking her with cream. (1855)
The cat and dog may kiss, yet are none the better friends. (1855)
A cat's walk: a little way and back. (1869)
When the cat of the house is black, the lasses of lovers will have no lack. (1878)
As busy as a cat in a tripe shop. (1890)
Like a cat in a bonfire, don't know which way to turn. (1895)
The trouble with a kitten is that eventually it becomes a cat. (1940)
Providence made the cat that man might have the pleasure of playing with the tiger. (1965)

17

CAT AUTHORITIES

OVER THE YEARS, many feline experts have devoted themselves to increasing our knowledge of the world of cats. Some have studied their natural history, others have laboured in the archives of cat literature, and still others have helped to develop the many exciting pedigree breeds we have today. Among them a few stand out as true authorities, individuals who have in one way or another made a major, original contribution to the subject.

FRANÇOIS-AUGUSTIN PARADIS DE MONCRIF

The French author, poet, musician, dramatist and actor, François-Augustin Paradis de Moncrif (1687–1770), has been justly described as 'the first genuine chronicler of cats'. His now famous book *Les Chats*, published in 1727, is the first complete volume seriously devoted to the subject. It consists of eleven letters to a Madame la M. de B★★ and ten poems.

The book was written to please his noble patrons. In it, he vigorously defends the cat against its many critics and persecutors: 'One has heard since the cradle that Cats are treacherous by nature, that they suffocate infants; that perhaps they are sorcerers. Succeeding reason may cry out in vain against these calumnies… You know, Madame,… there is none among the animals who can bear more brilliant titles than those of the Cat species.'

He ends the letters on an optimistic note: '…one day we shall see the merit of Cats generally recognized. It is impossible that in a nation as enlightened as our own the prejudice in this regard should prevail much longer over so reasonable a statement.'

Moncrif was described as witty, handsome, seductive and fastidious. The son of a Scottish mother and French father, he was a debonair figure at the court of Louis XV. However, when his cat book was published, Moncrif was lampooned and his ideas were met with ridicule. Savage skits and biting satires appeared. Two years later, when he was being admitted to the French Academy, a fellow Academician let a live cat loose at the ceremony. During Moncrif's maiden speech, the terrified cat miaowed pitifully and the audience of pompous Academicians mimicked its cries. Influenced by the

Two of the illustrations from Moncrif's Les Chats *showing (left) the tomb of a Parisian cat and (right) the sacred cat of Egypt*

ridicule he had to bear, Moncrif eventually withdrew *Les Chats* from circulation and from his collected works. The irony is that today all his other works – not to mention those of his fellow Academicians – are forgotten, while his little book in praise of cats is prized as the forerunner of modern feline literature.

Bibliography

1727. Moncrif, F-A. P. de. *Les Chats*. Gabriel-François Quilleau, Paris.
1961. *Moncrif's Cats*. Translated by Reginald Bretnor. Golden Cockerel Press, London. (Limited to 400 copies.)
1969. *Moncrif's Cats*. Translated by Reginald Bretnor. Barnes, New York. (A re-issue of the 1961 edition.)

CHAMPFLEURY

Champfleury was the pseudonym of the French author Jules Fleury-Husson (1821–1889), who wrote one of the most important cat books of the nineteenth century: *Les Chats; histoire – moeurs – observations – anecdotes*. It was translated into English by Frances Cashel Hoey and published by George Bell as *The Cat Past and Present*. A feline classic, it is one of the very first attempts to produce a factual, scholarly account of the domestic cat.

Bibliography

1869. Champfleury. *Les Chats; histoire – moeurs – observations – anecdotes.*
1885. Champfleury. Translated (with supplementary notes) by Mrs Cashel Hoey. *The Cat Past and Present*. Bell, London.

HARRISON WEIR

Journalist, author and artist, Harrison Weir (1824–1906) has justly been described as the 'father of the pedigree cat show'. The holding of the first major cat show – at Crystal Palace in 1871 – was entirely his idea. He also organized it and he and his brother were two of the three judges. There were 170 cats present, arranged in 25 classes, and the show proved so popular with the public that it started a whole new trend in competitive cat breeding, a trend that has grown and expanded to become a worldwide pursuit at the present time.

Commenting on his motives, he said: 'I conceived the idea that it would be well to hold "cat shows", so that the different breeds, colours, markings, etc. might be more carefully attended to, and the domestic cat, sitting in front of the fire, would then possess a beauty and attractiveness to its owner unobserved because uncultivated heretofore.'

Harrison Weir with a prize-winning Persian kitten at the Crystal Palace show

His 1889 book *Our Cats and all about them* is considered one of the early classics on the subject. In his *Who's Who* entry he listed as his recreation: 'no games of any sort at any time'.

Bibliography

1889 Weir, Harrison. *Our Cats and all about them; their varieties, habits, and management.* Tunbridge Wells: Clements and Co., Mount Pleasant.

ST GEORGE MIVART

Zoology lecturer, Dr St George Mivart (1827–1900), published the first major study of the anatomy and biology of the cat in 1881. Running to 557 pages, it was a milestone in the history of feline knowledge. Commenting on it in 1903, Frances Simpson wrote: 'The great scholar and eminent writer, St George Mivart, has given the world a wonderfully comprehensive work on the cat, and has used the maligned feline as his type for an introduction to the study of back-boned animals.'

Bibliography

1881. Mivart, St George. *The Cat. An introduction to the study of backboned animals especially mammals.* John Murray, London.

GORDON STABLES

One of the earliest of cat authors, Gordon Stables (1840–1910), a Berkshire doctor and well-known judge at the early cat shows, was the only person to write more than one serious book about cats in the nineteenth century. His style may have been patronizing, but he must be given credit for having been one of the few serious voices raised in defence of the cat in Victorian times.

Bibliography

1874. *Cats. Their Points and Characteristics*. Dean, London.

1876. *The Domestic Cat*. Routledge, London.

1877. *Friends in Fur. True Tales of Cat Life*. Dean, London.

1895. *Shireen and her Friends. Pages from the Life of a Persian Cat*. Jarrold, London.

1897. *Cats. Handbook to their classification and diseases*. Dean, London.

FRANCES SIMPSON

By the end of the nineteenth century, competitive cat shows had become established and great interest had arisen in the subject of pure lines of pedigree cats. In 1903, Frances Simpson, a prominent cat breeder, show manager and judge, produced a major reference work on the subject that was to have lasting value.

As recently as 1972, Claire Necker had special praise for Simpson's *The Book of the Cat*: 'Although dated, this book is still considered the most comprehensive on cat breeds, as least from the historic angle. A classic in its field.' In 1985, Grace Pond commented: '*The Book of the Cat* by Frances Simpson… is one of the most comprehensive books on the early days of the Cat Fancy that has ever been written. It has been published worldwide and is a never-ending source of interest.'

Bibliography

1902. Simpson, F. *Cats and all about them*. Isbister, London.

1903. Simpson, F. *The Book of the Cat*. Cassell, London.

1905. Simpson, F. *Cats for Pleasure and Profit*. Pitman, London.

GRACE POND

Grace Pond (1910–2002) is the most prolific of all cat authors, with more than twenty cat books to her credit. She was the Organizer of the UK National Cat Club Show, the largest cat show in the world, for forty years, from 1953 to 1993, and was responsible for introducing special classes for non-pedigree pet cats – a brave innovation for which she was strongly criticized. She has since been the president of many cat clubs, including the Governing Council of the Cat Fancy (GCCF). She was also famous as a breeder and as an international show judge. She gave up breeding in 1979, but continued to add to her long list of books about cats.

She was given her first cat – a Black Persian – when she was four years old and this began a lifelong involvement with long-haired cats, on which she became a world expert.

Bibliography

1959. *The Observer's Book of Cats*. Warne, London.

1962. *Cats*. Arco, New York.

1964. *Persian Cats*. Foyles, London.

1966. *Cat Lovers' Diary*. Museum Press, London.

1966. *The Perfect Cat Owner*. Museum Press, London.

1968. *The Long-haired Cats*. Arco, London.

1969. *Complete Cat Guide*. Pet Library, London.

1969. *The Batsford Book of Cats*. Batsford, London.

1970. (with Elizabeth Towe) *Cats*. Cassell, London.

1972. (with Catherine Ing) *Champion Cats of the World*. Harrap, London.

1972. (with Alison Ashford) *Rex, Abyssinian and Turkish Cats*. Gifford, London.

1972. (Editor) *The Complete Cat Encyclopedia*. Heinemann, London.

1974. (Editor) *The Cat Lover's Bedside Book*. Batsford, London.

1974. (with Muriel Calder) *The Longhaired Cat*. Batsford, London.

1976. (with Angela Sayer) *Cats*. Bartholomew, Edinburgh.

1977. (with Angela Sayer) *The Intelligent Cat*. Davis-Poynter, London

1979. (with Ivor Raleigh) *A Standard Guide to Cat Breeds*. Macmillan, London.

1980. *Pictorial Encyclopedia of Cats*. Rand McNally, New York.

1982. *The Cat. The Breeds, the Care and the Training*. Exeter Books, New York.

1983. *Longhaired Cats*. Batsford, London.
1985. (with Mary Dunnill) *Cat Shows and Successful Showing*. Blandford Press, Poole, Dorset.

PAUL LEYHAUSEN

One of the world's leading experts on the behaviour of small cat species, German ethologist Dr Paul Leyhausen's classic work, *Verhaltensstudien an Katzen*, was first published in 1956. The most detailed study ever made of feline behaviour, it surprisingly remained untranslated for almost a quarter of a century. Eventually it did appear in English in a greatly enlarged form in 1979, as *Cat Behavior*. Leyhausen's lengthy and meticulous observations provided many new insights into feline activities and established him as the foremost student of cat behaviour in the world.

Bibliography
1956. Leyhausen, P. *Verhaltensstudien an Katzen*. Paul Parey, Berlin.
1979. Leyhausen, P. *Cat behavior. The Predatory and Social Behavior of Domestic and Wild Cats*. Garland Press, New York.

CLAIRE NECKER

Chicago zoologist Claire Necker is the leading bibliographer on the topic of domestic cats. Her painstaking 1972 volume *Four Centuries of Cat Books* has become the classic reference work for the subject. It lists 2,293 titles and provides invaluable information for anyone researching a feline theme or assembling a feline library. Her 1973 sequel *The Cat's Got Our Tongue* is a fascinating, scholarly study of every word, phrase and proverb associated with cats.

Bibliography
1969. Necker, C. (Editor) *Cats and Dogs*. Barnes, New Jersey.
1970. Necker, C. *The Natural History of Cats*. Barnes, New Jersey.
1972. Necker, C. *Four Centuries of Cat Books. A Bibliography, 1570–1970*. Scarecrow Press, New Jersey.
1973. Necker, C. *The Cat's Got Our Tongue*. Scarecrow Press, New Jersey.
1974. Necker, C. (Editor) *Supernatural Cats*. Warner Books, New York.

ANGELA SAYER

Angela Sayer is the President of the Cat Association of Great Britain, Vice-President of the Cat Survival Trust, an international show judge, a major figure in cat breeding, and a breed innovator, having introduced several new breeds to Britain. She has also organized the annual Kensington Cat Show, been editor of *Cat World* magazine, run a feline quarantine station and organized wildlife safaris to Africa. In addition, she is a professional animal photographer (under the name Solitaire) and has run her own company: Animal Graphics Ltd. She has written many books on feline subjects (some as Angela Sayer, others as Angela Rixon) including the following:

Bibliography

1976. Pond, G and Sayer, A. *Cats*. John Bartholomew, Edinburgh.
1977. Pond, G and Sayer, A. *The Intelligent Cat*. Davis-Poynter, London.
1979. Sayer, A. *The Encyclopedia of the Cat*. Octopus Books, London.
1982. Sayer, A. *The World of Cats*. Optimum Books, London.
1983. Sayer, A. *Cats: A Guide to Breeding and Showing*. Batsford, London.
1984. Sayer, A. *The Complete Book of the Cat*. Octopus Books, London.
1990. Sayer, A (co-author). *The Noble Cat*. Merehurst, London.
1995. Rixon, A. *The Illustrated Encyclopedia of Cat Breeds*. Blandford, London.

GEORGE SCHALLER

George Schaller was the first modern zoologist to make prolonged, analytical observations of big cats in the wild. His pioneering studies of tigers in India, lions in Africa and snow leopards in the Himalayas became models for the many field investigations that were to follow. Before he began his work in the 1950s, observations of big game animals were largely anecdotal or personal. Most of them relied on the experiences of scouts, trackers and hunters, or of those who had enjoyed the company of a tame or captive animal. They had learned a great deal, but it was not organized, systematically collected information.

Schaller brought a new, objective approach to the subject and his reports gave us the first detailed information about the life history and behaviour of the greatest members of the cat family. It was his goal to reveal the animals as they really were, rather than as human fears, emotions and sentimentality had painted them in the past. As he put it: 'When humans observe an animal they mainly see the fiction they have invented for it.' Schaller's aim was to replace that fiction with fact.

Bibliography

1967. Schaller, G. *The Deer and the Tiger*. University of Chicago Press, Illinois.
1971. Schaller, G and Selsam, M E. *The Tiger. Its Life in the Wild*. World's Work, London.
1972. Schaller, G. *The Serengeti Lion*. University of Chicago Press, Illinois.
1972. Schaller, G. *Serengeti, Kingdom of Predators*. Knopf, New York.
1973. Schaller, G. *Golden Shadows, Flying Hooves*. Knopf, New York.
1977. Schaller, G. *Mountain Monarchs*. University of Chicago Press, Illinois.

ROGER TABOR

His field studies of the behaviour of feral cats in a city environment resulted in one of the modern classics of feline literature. In addition to his research into urban ecology, he also began broadcasting in the early 1970s, covering a wide range of feline topics. In 1990 he travelled the world in search of new information about domestic cats, for his BBC TV series *The Rise of the Cat*. In 1995 he presented a further TV series for the BBC, *Understanding Cats*, dealing with feline behaviour.

Bibliography

1983. Tabor, R. *The Wild Life of the Domestic Cat*. Arrow Books, London.
1991. Tabor, R. *Cats: The Rise of the Cat*. BBC Books, London.
1995. Tabor, R. *Understanding Cats*. David and Charles, Newton Abbot, Devon.

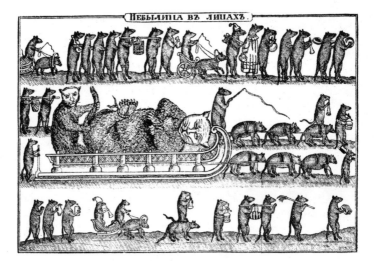

'The End of the Cat'
A Russian caricature of the funeral of Peter the Great. He is depicted as a cat
and the funeral is being conducted by mice.